DATE DUE

~~Nov 28~~			
~~Aug 22~~			

MOVING AND REORGANIZING A LIBRARY

MOVING AND REORGANIZING A LIBRARY

❖

Marianna S. Wells
and
Rosemary Young

Gower

~~~ublished by
~Publishing Limited
~ower House
~Croft Road
~Aldershot
~shire GU11 3HR
~England

Gower
Old Post Road
Brookfield
Vermont 05036
USA

Marianna Wells and Rosemary Young have asserted their right under the
Copyright, Designs and Patents Act 1988 to be identified as the
authors of this work

British Library Cataloguing in Publication Data
Wells, Marianna
  Moving and reorganizing a library
  1. Libraries – Planning
  I. Title   II. Young, Rosemary
  025.1

ISBN 0 566 07701 9

Library of Congress Cataloging-in-Publication Data
Wells, Marianna S. (Marianna Salzbrunn), 1929–
  Moving and reorganizing a library / by Marianna S. Wells and
Rosemary M. Young.
     p.   cm.
  Includes index.
  ISBN 0-566-07701-9
  1. Library moving—United States.   2. Stack management
(Libraries)—United States.   I. Young, Rosemary M., 1950–   .
II. Title.
Z703.5W45   1997
025.8′1—dc20   96–30371
                                                            CIP

Typeset in Garamond by Raven Typesetter, Chester
and printed in Great Britain by Biddles Ltd, Guildford.

The art of progress
is to preserve order amid change and
to preserve change amid order.

Alfred North Whitehead (1861–1947)
Harvard scholar, mathematician and
philosopher

Dedicated to
Thomas Steven Wells
and
June and Russell Young

CONTENTS

LIST OF FIGURES

PREFACE

For librarians, planning a library move is a once in a lifetime experience. No wonder we are intimidated and overwhelmed when faced with the prospect of having to take on such a daunting assignment. A good way to overcome an obstacle is to break it into smaller, more manageable parts. This book intends to do just that, as it guides the uninitiated along the path of planning and executing a move from its inception to its completion.

The book begins by examining reasons why a move might be contemplated. It goes on to pose two possible solutions for a library which has outgrown its present facility. One solution is to expand and modernize the library by designing a new facility. The other is to choose from a variety of alternative solutions that could meet the needs of a library.

Part One of the book offers a blueprint on planning and moving a library into enhanced quarters. Its approach is chronological in the sense that the sequence of the chapters replicates the planning process, in the order in which it ought to be undertaken. Its chapters provide practical suggestions on what to do before, during and after a move. Part Two offers alternatives to a new library that will find resonance among those unable to raise the capital funding needed for a new construction or renovation project.

What is the background of the authors that would qualify them to put together such a book? Both writers are librarians with the University of Cincinnati, Marianna Wells is Head of the combined Geology/Physics Library, with a collection of 100 000 volumes and a collection of over 100 000 topographic maps. It is one of several branch libraries in the University of Cincinnati Libraries' System. Its mission is to support the teaching and research efforts of the university's faculty and students in the pursuit of doctoral and master's degree programmes, by providing timely access to scholarly publications in the disciplines of geology and physics.

Rosemary Young is the Head of the OMI College of Applied Science Library with a collection of approximately 50 000 volumes. The Ohio Mechanics Institute, as it was once called, was established in 1828. It was the first technical institute west of the Alleghenies and the sixth in the United States. The University of Cincinnati acquired the OMI College of Applied Science in 1969 as the university's sixteenth college. The college offers baccalaureate level degrees (Bachelor of Science, etc.) in the engineering technologies. In 1989, the college moved from its inner-city campus to a picturesque campus overlooking the Ohio River.

The authors' expertise is based on experience. Each was charged with drawing up plans to renovate and reorganize their libraries and to move their collections into new quarters in 1989/1990. The projects incorporated considerations of spatial arrangements of service point and the housing of their collections, readers and staff.

Marianna Wells' assignment also included a mandate to merge two science libraries previously located at separate institutes. The combined library was to be housed in a building previously occupied by the university's bookshop. A particular challenge of the project was the merger of a widely dispersed periodical collection located at various storage facilities. An online database was created to carry out this objective. Several other activities took place during the three years preceding the transfer in an effort to review and prime the collection prior to the move. A weeding and conservation project was carried out. The collections' holdings were converted to data file. An inventory was undertaken and online records updated to reflect changes. In anticipation of a modern security system, physical volumes were tattletaped – tattletape is magnetized tape that is inserted into books. At exits, libraries have an alarm system that is activated when a book is not officially checked out and, at that time, de-magnetized – and barcoded, and their barcodes linked to online records.

Rosemary Young's experience was similar in some aspects but different in others. Her library collection, steeped in the history of Cincinnati's industrial past, but neglected over the years, required extensive priming prior to the move. The collection was inventoried for the first time in decades. A large-scale deselection project was undertaken. The collection was reclassified from the Dewey to the Library of Congress subject classification system and its records converted to data file. Clean-up and conservation efforts were undertaken. Resources were updated. All of this was completed in a three-year time frame in preparation for the move.

The challenge each of the authors faced was different yet similar. It became apparent to them that, although every library is unique as defined by its size, clientele and character, there are common denominators that are shared by all libraries in the planning and moving of collections.

It is this commonality of interests and concerns that the authors wished to present in their book with the expectation that the reader will be able to apply useful elements to his or her own setting. Since the authors have gained their experience from working in the United States, measurements, specifications and the like tend to be expressed in terms peculiar to the US. The authors have used them only where they felt their inclusion would be helpful to illustrate a point. It is anticipated that the reader will explore appropriate equivalents if, and where, desirable. Online sources tend to be international in character and are familiar to librarians worldwide.

Marianna S. Wells
Rosemary Young

ACKNOWLEDGEMENTS

I have been intrigued for many years with the intricacies and logistics of planning a library. After a highly successful conclusion of a renovation and moving project, guides I had developed stayed in my files for possible use in a future undertaking. Now the undertaking has become this book.

Since the impetus for writing this book sprang from a specific experience, I would like to thank those individuals whose assistance had been vital to that project's success. Foremost I am indebted to F. William Louden, then Assistant Dean of Library Planning, the team member with whom I worked most closely. William Louden is now Director of the University of Evansville Libraries in Evansville, Indiana, USA. I am grateful beyond words to Ellen Shostak Rosenzon, the designer of the database which turned out to be the key to moving and integrating our large journal collection. I would like to acknowledge with gratitude my staff member Cathy Minix Luhn, who cheerfully and tirelessly performed endless calculations, helped with site preparation and supervised the large contingent of student helpers during the move. Another person on the team was the Geology Librarian, Richard A. Spohn.

There have been a number of people who were instrumental in seeing this book come to fruition and I am grateful to each and every one of them. I wish to thank Stefan A. Funke, Doctor of Medicine and computer aficionado, for the computer-generated diagrams. Thomas Steven Wells, my son, encouraged me to put my experience on paper. Ruth Auckenthaler Hamilton, a cousin, urged me for years to try my hand at writing. Lydia Salzbrunn Funke, my sister provided me with resolve when needed. Margaret Talbert lent me her support and encouragement.

Among my colleagues at the University of Cincinnati, I would like to mention my co-author Rosemary Young whose considerable expertise contributed to the book's conception and design. I sincerely appreciate the support and counsel of Dr Bernard Goodman, Professor of Physics, who was a supporter of this endeavour from the start. I wish to acknowledge Jason Jones for contributing the computer-generated tables. My colleague, English bibliographer Rosemary Franklin, was generous enough to proof-read the book with an eye to style and syntax. Finally, I would like to thank Peter Dale of the British Library, for his advice on UK/European equivalents to US terms, measurements and specifications.

Marianna Salzbrunn Wells
11/01/95

I would like to acknowledge the assistance of Toby Heidtman and his team in the physical move of the OMI College of Applied Science collection. I give special thanks to my staff and volunteers involved in the move of the OMI College of Applied Science Library: Carol O'Brien, Cheryl Calhoun, Steve Karoly, Anne Abate and George Maley.

Rosemary M. Young
12/01/95

INTRODUCTION

WHY MOVE?

The rapid development of information technologies has deeply affected libraries in the past 20 years giving rise to the assumption that space for print collections is going to be less of an issue than it has been in the past. So far, this premise has not been borne out. Television has not replaced the cinema, the cinema has not replaced reading, access to library sources via computer has not replaced the classical library.

Technologies continue to enrich and nourish rather than curtail publication output. More books and journals are published worldwide than ever before. Bowker's *Annual of Library and Trade Almanac* cites a 392 per cent increase in publishing output from 1970 to 1990 (35th edn, p. 480, 1990) and growth in libraries has continued unabated.

THE DILEMMA OF SPACE

As a consequence, space continues to be a problem which librarians have to solve: space for library materials, space for readers, space for new technology. Although alternative solutions to space problems have found acceptance, new construction and renovation projects for libraries have endured.

STACKS

The most frequent cause for a move or reorganization is overcrowding of stack space. Since growth of collections is exponential, even a seemingly modest annual expansion rate requires considerable extra stack space.

1

Older library facilities were not designed to accommodate the prodigious publication growth of the last decades. An expedient answer to satisfy the demand for space as numbers of publications increase typically has been to eliminate seating in favour of adding a couple of book shelves here and there. But by giving temporary relief to one problem another predicament was created.

READER SPACES

When collection growth has overtaken space previously set aside for readers, accommodation of library users will eventually become a driving force for change. Moreover, colleges have seen an increase in student enrolment, especially in commuter populations.

Contrary to common belief, the number of commuters in a college population will not decrease the demand for seating in a library but rather increase it. Students desire to make efficient use of the time interval between lectures. Others arrive early to make sure they can find convenient parking. Older students with families often prefer the library over their noisier student residence or homes. Whether for study or research, libraries are generally sought out for their atmosphere. When libraries can accommodate books but not the people who use them a situation has come about that needs to be addressed.

NEW TECHNOLOGIES

No one can properly evaluate space requirements without including a discussion about the new technology. Librarians who wish to give access to technological innovations will want to provide leadership in defining and implementing new programmes that help users to make the fullest use of such resources. This requires space and an infrastructure for necessary equipment and service points.

ONLINE SYSTEMS

New technologies are changing the way libraries are run. The venerable, once indispensable card catalogue has made room for online catalogues. The term 'online' refers to a system in which input data enters the computer directly from a point of origin, usually a databank, and output data is directly transmitted to where it is used. An online catalogue can become part of an interconnected group of computers that are linked together for the purpose of sharing data files. Thus, an online catalogue provides the potential of networking with catalogues at other institutions, giving broadened user access to library sources beyond the parent institution. Regional, national and even international library consortia list their library collections online. WorldCat offers global access to the collections of 20 000 libraries worldwide.

CD-ROM TECHNOLOGY

Information found in indices, abstracts or encyclopaedic works is now usually accessible via CD-ROM. CD-ROM stands for Compact Disk-Read Only Memory. It provides data storage in optical form on a disk that uses a laser to read information from the disk. Library users prefer them to print indexes because they can do their searching while sitting at a computer work station. A number of encyclopaedias are now on the market in CD-ROM format; and *Books in Print*, that much-used publication source with its tiny letters in dark grey on only slightly lighter-coloured grey paper, can now be tossed aside in favour of *BIP Plus Online*.

OTHER MEDIA

Serious consideration is being given to the inclusion of multimedia and audiovisual services in today's libraries. Should not the student who is studying Shakespeare have the opportunity to choose between either a print version of Hamlet or a disk or a video?

Library clients aware of technical innovations in information science expect them to be incorporated into regional and local libraries. But often, older facilities simply are not suitable to accommodate new equipment without some major renovation.

STAFF

Every time the library offers a new service, it must be viewed not only from the perspective of space for tables and work stations for equipment but also of proper staff placement. Not all library users are skilled with the use of computers or the wide variety of software products. In the absence of standardized command language, library users tend to have questions about search terminology and equipment use. Libraries nowadays offer so much, and in so many different versions, that users require the assistance of an information professional. Is there room within the information hub to accommodate one or more staff stations? An accurate assessment of the problem and its possible solutions is the first step in solving a problem.

MOVE OF THE PARENT INSTITUTION

Plans for the move of a library might be put into motion by a parent organization's decision to have a new building constructed to house a department or college. If there is a branch library that serves the needs of the faculty and students in that unit, chances are the library will be identified to be part of the impending construction of and move to a new building. It is a lucky break for the librarian if this happens. Indeed, it was the reason for the move into new quarters for the libraries for which both authors are department heads.

PART ONE

PLANNING A NEW FACILITY

❖

An ideal solution to library space problems is the construction of a new library facility or the renovation of an existing one to become effectively a new library.

In spite of the fact that capital improvement funding has been more difficult to obtain in today's economic climate, construction projects for libraries have not yet passed into oblivion. The demand to provide more space for library materials and services continues unabated.

What follows is a guide for planning and moving a library into new or renovated quarters. It addresses how to plan, design, prepare and implement a move to a new facility from the time of the project's inception to its completion. Considerations include how to get started, how to create a library layout that serves the demands of the modern library user, how to optimize access to new technologies and how to apply standards for space requirements and relevant codes for floor load capacity, lighting, heating, ventilating and air conditioning.

A chapter is devoted to training issues, as staff training plays a prominent part in both the preliminary planning process as well as the individual project phases, like the assessment of collection size and the implementation of the move. The impact of change on personnel as a phenomenon that, with some foresight, can be managed, will be addressed.

Selecting a moving company, reviewing the collection before the count, establishing collection size, predicting collection growth and site preparation prior to the move are discussed in depth as they are the cornerstone to a successful move.

Not included in this book are guidelines for chosing a site for a new library, exterior designs and structures, exterior landscaping, parking needs and the like. Such topics are addressed in detail in other references, most

5

notably *Planning Academic and Research Library Buildings* by Keyes D. Metcalf (1986), and are cited in the References at the end of the book.

1

PRELIMINARY CONSIDERATIONS

NEEDS ASSESSMENT

The first step in planning a new library is to formulate an assessment of needs. Needs are characteristic to a particular setting. The requirement for upgrading a facility will be based, among others, on the issues discussed in the Introduction, which examined reasons for a reorganization or move.

PROJECT ENDORSEMENT

The needs assessment has to be endorsed by the parent organization. Obtaining the commitment of the organization is vital for seeking funding. The case is usually made in the form of a written proposal to be submitted for approval.

PROPOSAL

A proposal of this nature will state the mission of the library, its past history and future direction. It will outline the library's functional requirements, structural requirements, specific design features, figures, a cost estimate and a time schedule. This information will be the cornerstone for raising funding for the project. The proposal's elements and other considerations shall be examined in the following as a preparation for writing the proposal.

MISSION STATEMENT

What are the typical functions of libraries? It can be said that the mission of a modern library is to provide the full range of communication and information services necessary to carry out the goals and duties of a library. College libraries support and enhance programmes of instruction, learning, research, and publication. Public libraries provide a service and accumulate books, media and other formats of interest to local residents. The focus of special or commercial libraries is to fill specific needs that arise in connection with related problems shared by a given clientele.

FUTURE DEVELOPMENTS

What are the likely future developments in libraries? Although the book has remained king and continues to be the principal source of learning, printed materials no longer provide the only access to information. A plan for a new library must take into consideration flexibility and adaptation to future electronic library services.

BRAINSTORMING IDEAS

What new trends should be incorporated into a new design? What are the characteristics of the specific library to be redesigned? What does the client want from the library? Begin the process of brainstorming early enough to allow time for self-preparation.

CONDUCT USER SURVEYS

Seek the input of users, colleagues and staff. Conduct a survey to find out about user patterns, views and preferences for short-term and long-term goals.

SEARCH FOR RELEVANT LITERATURE

Peruse pertinent literature about planning a new facility. Sources on library planning and moving are given in the References at the end of this book. Sign on to the listserv for library planning on the Internet: LIBPLN–L. Learn about new trends in the library profession.

CONTACT COLLEAGUES FOR ADVICE

Pick up creative ideas by visiting other libraries. Whenever possible, take advantage of library tours locally as well as in other cities when attending conferences. Seek the counsel of colleagues who have planned new facilities and a move and get their advice on dos and don'ts.

WRITING A PROGRAMME STATEMENT

Planning a library necessitates orderly, well-thought out strategies, chronicled in writing. Such a document is commonly referred to as a Programme Statement.

The purpose of the Programme Statement is manifold. It provides library administrators with the necessary justification to initiate changes, it serves as the basis for the project's budget proposal and it informs the architects about the desirable layout of the library, service areas and specific space needs. The Programme Statement also serves as the official authority concerning planning and development. It will be consulted before, during and after the move has been completed.

The Programme Statement should cover the following topics.

PROGRAMME STATEMENT

General description and impact statement

○ review of library goals
○ brief history of the library
○ analysis of past inadequacies
○ future scope of operations

Distribution of space requirements

○ collections
○ reader spaces
○ new technology
○ equipment

Design elements

○ spatial relationships, that is the relative position of library spaces

Description of specific space requirements

○ entrance lobby
○ circulation desk
○ information hub/reference area
○ reader areas

○   staff room
○   library office(s)
○   bibliographic instruction

General building considerations

○   codes and standards
○   floor load considerations
○   lighting
○   wiring
○   heating/ventilating/air conditioning
○   security
○   signage

Net space requirements (See Figure 1.1 for sample.)

A	READER SPACES			
•	Study carrels	$20@30$ ft^2	=	600 ft^2
•	Reserve and general study area	$40@30$	=	$1\,200$
•	Media area	$6@48$	=	288
•	Current unbound periodicals	$4@30$	=	120
•	Faculty reading room	$8@30$	=	240
•	Map area	$5@30$	=	150
•	Reference	$8@30$	=	240
•	Conference room (no formula)			300
•	Terminals/work stations	$6@30$	=	180
•	Faculty study (no formula)			100
⇒	Total			3418 ft^2

B	STACK AREA	
•	Stacks	$12\,200$ ft^2
•	Map area	830
•	Media area	350
•	Reference	255
•	Current unbound periodicals	250
•	Faculty reading room	200
⇒	Total	$14\,085$ ft^2

C	SERVICE AREA	
•	Circulation and reserve	500 ft^2
•	Offices	500
•	Workroom	500
•	Reference	400
•	Map area	50
⇒	Total	1950 ft^2

GRAND TOTAL, NET SPACE REQUIREMENTS $19\,453$ ft^2

FIGURE 1.1   EXAMPLE OF NET SPACE REQUIREMENTS FOR A LIBRARY

FORMAT OF PROGRAMME STATEMENT

The format of the Programme Statement should be brief but to the point. The introductory statements regarding mission, history, and so on, should be succinct while the descriptive part should be appropriately detailed. The following are examples.

Circulation

This area should be located at the library entrance. The circulation desk should be a major service point. It must be large enough to house several staff members to handle heavy demand at peak periods of use. For example

Service area:	400 sq. ft.
Photocopier:	100 sq. ft.
Net space requirements:	500 sq. ft.

Work room

The work room should be adjacent to the circulation desk and allow staff to have a behind-the-scenes overview of the routines performed at this public station so that assistance can be available at peak periods. It should be adjacent to the lift. The work room can be set up as a typical office area, with lockers and the appropriate number of work stations. For example

Staff: 6 @ 100 sq. ft. each = 600 sq. ft.
Net space requirements: 600 sq. ft.

Study areas

This may be an area set aside for cursory use, located near the entrance foyer, or a more serious study area which should be shielded from noise. For example

40 reader stations @ 30 sq.ft. each	=	1 200 sq. ft.
1 photocopier @ 100 sq.ft.	=	100 sq. ft.
Net space requirements :		1 300 sq. ft.

Future chapters will provide the basis for the description of the new facility. Useful tips for a variety of specific space requirements in libraries, given in both the imperial and the metric scale, can be found in Metcalf (1986).

MAKING A COST ESTIMATE

The amount of funding is dependent upon the size, specificity and largess of the projects and its supporters. Budget estimates (see Chapter 4) would cover the cost for

O   land on which the property is located, the exterior of the building, parking lots, landscaping;

○   fees for architectural and engineering support;
○   interior design;
○   new furnishings;
○   equipment to support new technology;
○   stack shelving, including compact shelving;
○   technical requirements such as heating, air ventilation and air con-
        ditioning, floor load capacity, wiring, lighting, carpeting, acoustics,
        and so on;
○   signage;
○   moving expenses;
○   wages for helpers and overtime pay for staff.

For projects with a large budget, it may be possible and/or necessary to hire
a consultant.

BID PROPOSALS

Any proposal that is subject to a bid must be specific in its outline of costs
and what the money is to pay for. The outline must be finalized in writing
and no changes made unless formally discussed and approved by all
involved parties as modifications affect the budget. If the bid comes back
higher than anticipated, the project must be re-evaluated as a whole and in
its particulars if the project is to be kept within fiscal limits.

SMALL PROJECTS

It may not seem necessary to make a cost estimate if the project is small. Any
project that uses funding obtained from an official source requires account-
ability. Regardless of the scope of the project, it is necessary to establish a
cost estimate to make sure that monies are properly accounted for and that
funding does not run out before the project is completed.

ESTABLISHING A TIMETABLE

How much time should be set aside for early planning depends on the
scope of the project. A minor move will require a few weeks of preparation,
while a renovation project will entail anything from months to a couple of
years. Laying plans for the building of a new library facility could well
extend over several years prior to the onset of construction. But, regardless
of the size of the project, do not postpone planning any part of it until the
last minute. Being ahead of the project means that unanticipated surprises
can be dealt with in a timely fashion.

A timetable for the actual project is the next step. Assume that the implementation of the project is completed a year hence. Put down that date on the left side of the ledger. Then work from right to left, filling in dates or time periods for items/steps in the order in which they have to be completed, for example, 'one week prior to moving, label empty shelves in new facility'. Do the same for all steps, such as when to map the move, when to engage the removal company, when to hire assistants, when to train assistants, when to have the Programme Statement approved, when to have the budget approved, when to write the Programme Statement, when to review the collection, when to commence project planning.

Examine the timetable and see whether it looks reasonable and suitable. Make sure that enough time has been allotted for the various preparatory stages. Be generous with time allowances rather than stingy unless you are pressed for time in which case you need a tight schedule that is followed rigorously. An example of a timetable is shown in Figure 1.2 overleaf.

Dates: to be filled in as necessary	Activity
	Notification of impending move.
	Appointment of library's facility planner (the person in charge of overall library planning project). Library's facility planner will meet with architects regularly.
	Select move supervisor and/or move committee.
	User survey to assess needs of library's constituents.
	Search literature for relevant articles on planning a new facility and a move.
	Contact colleagues who have planned new facilities and made library moves for advice/support.
	Begin writing Programme Statement.
	Begin communication with library constituents and library staff regarding impact of impending library move. Communications will take place throughout process.
	Prepare collection as time permits: ○ weeding ○ inventory ○ binding ○ conservation ○ cleaning.
	Count collection after inventory and weeding completed.
	Estimate collection growth and shelving needs.
	Complete Programme Statement.
	Prepare orders for necessary shelving, new furniture, and equipment. (New furniture should be ordered six months prior to moving date.)
	Begin collecting addresses of all institutions, individuals, publishers, and vendors who will need to be notified of address changes.

FIGURE 1.2   TIMETABLE FOR PLANNING A MOVE

	Continue having periodic meetings with architect.
	Make periodic visits to new facility to insure all work is to specifications.
	Interview removal firms.
	Check references of removal firms.
	Make decision and sign contract with removal firm.
	Map placement of furniture and equipment in new facility using blueprints or other scaled layout.
	Map shelves for placement of collection.
	Make arrangements for refinishing and repair of old furniture to be moved.
	Make arrangements with service contract holders for moving and recalibration of equipment.
	Advertise for extra help, volunteers, or temporary staff to assist with move.
	Train library staff involved in move.
	Label shelves at new facility (approximately one week prior to move).
	Mark furniture and equipment that is to be moved and furniture and equipment that is to stay behind or be discarded. (Colour-coding is recommended.)
	Post mappings of each area at the new facility to assist move teams and movers.
	Last minute meeting and instructions to move teams.
	The move.
	Shakedown.
	Celebrate and recognize efforts of all involved in making the move successful.

FIGURE 1.2   *Concluded*

2

BLUEPRINT FOR A LIBRARY DESIGN

This chapter explains how to design a layout that considers the nature of interrelated library functions. It also takes a look at technical criteria as they apply to libraries.

GENERAL REQUIREMENTS

Library space is divided between public service points, reader spaces, staff stations, and stacks. Whenever and wherever possible, plan in terms of open spaces rather than walled-in areas. In today's rapidly changing techno-logical environment, libraries need to anticipate constant recurrence of and adjustment to innovations and open space lends itself more efficiently to future modifications. Make a thoughtful and thorough determination of how much space is required, where and why. Examine the various functions the library carries out and to what purpose. Use this opportunity to create an atmosphere both inviting and user-friendly.

FIRST IMPRESSIONS

Libraries tend to be intimidating to the uninitiated. The first thing a person should observe upon entering the library is that libraries are in the business of providing service. An information desk should be prominently placed within the first line of sight. Staff this desk with a person who communicates well with the public. Let attractive signage and a floor plan direct the user to specific parts of the library. Some people would rather follow signs than ask questions. In a smaller library operation, arrange for the library desk to be the first thing a person encounters upon entering.

Find ways to spruce up the entrance, to make it look attractive. A bulletin board with announcements of coming lectures, workshops, meetings and other notices of interest to the primary clientele would work, but do not let expired notices stay on beyond their date. Glass cases might exhibit fossils in a geology library, old maps in a map library, prints or paintings in an art library. But even a display of colourful dust jackets from new books can liven up the entrance. Plan for these elements in your new facility.

USE PATTERNS

An obvious way to make a library inviting is to tailor the design to reflect its distinctive use and purpose. Individual libraries have their own character-istic traffic patterns and often necessitate an arrangement more appropriate to one library but not to another. Thus, the layout of service points, the dis-play and arrangement of the collection, the grouping of reader spaces and their overall number, the extent and intensity of reference services, the need for special equipment are all subject to the specific needs and demands of your library.

USER CATEGORIES

A well-designed library is more than an attractive looking showcase. It is a place that will be used by a particular clientele for a particular purpose. Familiarity with the needs of one's clientele is the key to a good space lay-out.

Public libraries

Public libraries aim to benefit a large and varied clientele with a variety of backgrounds, ages and demands. The size of the community and whether it is urban or rural will determine its make-up. There is often a focus on children and librarians provide children's hours in an area where reading aloud would not be distracting to other library users. A mix of formats that includes music records or compact disks (CDs) is typically available in public libraries and requires tables with record and CD players and head-sets.

Research libraries

Research libraries serve a highly specialized clientele whose library use demands concentration and quietude. Several references are usually con-sulted and, therefore, study tables should be large enough to accommodate the simultaneous use of many sources.

College libraries

College libraries support both teaching and research curricula in an academic institution. Study use in such libraries tends to be varied. Librarians need to consider transitory as well as focused use. Transitory use and its traffic should be confined to a somewhat limited area, such as the entrance foyer, where the coming and going is not disturbing to the more serious library users for whom study space should be set aside within stack areas.

Special libraries

Special libraries typically serve commercial or industrial concerns where library holdings tend to be small but service intensive. The term special libraries is elusive enough to call for an example or two to demonstrate the point.

Law libraries   Law libraries serve specialized professionals in firms that are willing to pay for online searches as part of the cost that can be passed on to a client. Lawyers demand instant access to the pertinent legal databases. This translates into enough computer work stations to serve the resident lawyer population and online subscriptions to pertinent databases, such as Lexis or Westlaw. Access must be available at more than one work station. The company account must be set up to consider multiple simultaneous usage.

Medical libraries   Zana C. Etter discusses in her article 'Impact of Curriculum Revision on Media Collection', (*Special Libraries 86*:83–90, 1995) what sets medical libraries apart from other special libraries. Medical libraries rely on audiovisual support in the form of videodisks for case studies of patients or curricula in, for example, pathology. The major challenge for a medical librarian is to provide enough computer time for students. Medical school curricula tend to dictate what the library purchases and require that the information, which may no longer be current after five years, is constantly updated and always state of the art. In such a setting, the librarian might consider a separate area with an abundant number of computer stations, surrounded by shelving containing videodisks sorted by curricula or by subject for use by medical students, housemen (interns), faculty.

SPATIAL RELATIONSHIPS

The unique use which the primary clientele makes of a particular library tends to determine the interrelationship of a space in a layout.

Good public relations result when planners pay attention to ease of use. A successful design will consider the logical relationship between information services and professional information providers. Desks and offices of public

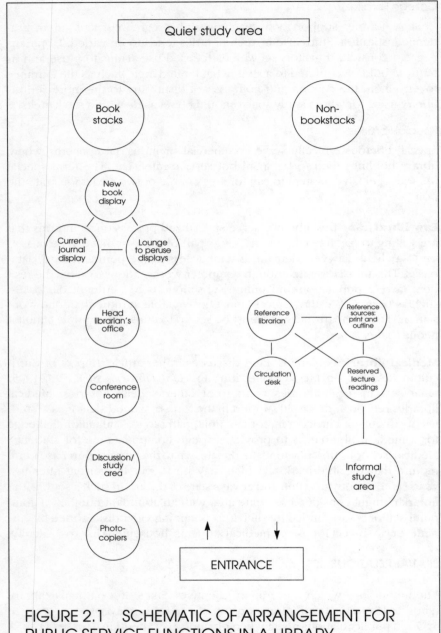

FIGURE 2.1   SCHEMATIC OF ARRANGEMENT FOR PUBLIC SERVICE FUNCTIONS IN A LIBRARY

service librarians should be in proximity to public information centres and their accoutrement. Figure 2.1 provides a schematic overview of the spatial relationship or relative positioning of library areas' spaces to one another and their interactive nature. The figure represents a conceptualization rather than a design layout. It shows that areas of high activity should be located near the entrance of the library to minimize noise elsewhere in the library. It explains how public services need be clustered around one or more desks staffed by librarians so that users can interact with service providers. It presents reader areas segregated by types of use. It indicates that stacks for books and journals can be relegated to areas where no staff desks tend to be situated.

SPECIFIC NEEDS

CIRCULATION DESK

Most appropriately located in the vicinity of the public entrance/exit of a library, the circulation desk tends to be the heart of library activities. A custom-made circulation counter is always the perfect, if costly, answer. Nowadays, companies specializing in library furniture mass-produce modular sections that can be mixed and matched to specifications. The advantage of modular furniture is lesser cost and greater flexibility. The sections usually include a book return, electrical connections and behind the counter desk space.

Give thought to what functions staff are to perform in addition to circulation duties. The stand-up counter version is most convenient for users who can place books on the counter top and write while standing. However, if staff are expected to perform other work when there is a lull in public service, select one of the modular sections with a secretarial desk.

ENTRANCE

A single entrance/exit to and from the library will greatly enhance the safety and protection of users, library materials and equipment. An electronic security system should be installed at the entrance/exit. It is convenient to have the detection system within sight of the circulation desk so that staff can communicate with a user should the alarm buzzer sound. Allow for a distance of ten feet between the security system and the electronic checkout system to avoid interference which occurs when different kinds of electronic equipment are in proximity of each other.

REFERENCE RESOURCE CENTRE

Reference resource centres are information hubs where a client can be served in a variety of ways. The centre should provide a clustering of access services. Figure 2.2 is a schematic of such a clustering of services. In addition to traditional print reference materials and lecture resources, the hub should provide access points to local and remote online resources and catalogues as well as interlibrary loan and document delivery services so that users can request books and articles not available locally. The availability of photocopiers and faxes within the hub would prove convenient for both the information seeker and the information provider.

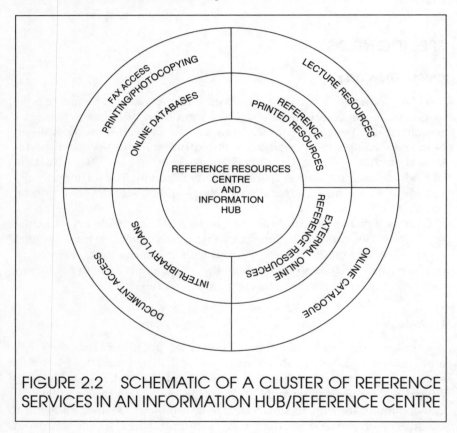

FIGURE 2.2   SCHEMATIC OF A CLUSTER OF REFERENCE SERVICES IN AN INFORMATION HUB/REFERENCE CENTRE

A key element in space planning is the location of the Reference Resource Centre. Its placement needs to satisfy several criteria. It must be strategically located so that it can be readily seen by incoming users. It needs to be close to both electronic and conventional reference sources. And the last and most important criterion is that there be room for flexibility in the way the hub is placed so that, should the original placement have to be changed, this can be accomplished with a minimum of cost. With technologies reinventing themselves with daunting regularity, librarians constantly re-evaluate their ideas on the services that they offer. A new situation may require changes in how the area is to be arranged. This will make more sense, perhaps, if a word is added on what installation of an electronic reference area entails.

INTEGRATED LIBRARY SYSTEMS

Integrated library systems require communication lines to transmit, via wire or telephone circuit, digital data by way of a pulse or signal from a remote station to a computer. Installation of equipment, incoming telecommunication lines and telephone connections has to consider proper wire management (see page 28).

Keep the hub at a distance of at least ten feet to safeguard electronic equipment from strong magnetic forces such as those contained in a security system or the equipment used to de-magnetize tattletaped books upon checkout and re-magnetize them upon return. The set-up you choose should have the potential for alterations and additions to the hub without having to relocate the whole arrangement.

LIBRARIAN'S OFFICE

The librarian's office should be readily accessible to both users and staff. There are a surprising number of libraries where offices of library officials are located on top floors away from the ebb and flow of the public. Such ill-advised placement is a detriment to good public relations. That holds true particularly in a smaller library, where the librarian should have a clear view of the action so that assistance can be given during peak times. The librarian's office is one of the few closed office areas we recommend. Meetings and one-to-one interaction with staff or users require privacy.

STAFF AREAS

Staff areas should be designed to facilitate work flow. It is a good idea to conduct an ergonomic study with close staff participation to determine how staff perform their work, which specific tasks are done by whom, how much time is spent on each, and what tools (computers, files) are required to accomplish these functions. The study will assist in determining areas for optimal staff placement.

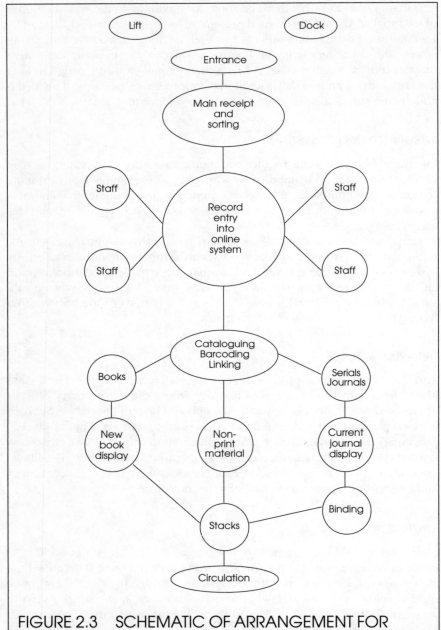

FIGURE 2.3   SCHEMATIC OF ARRANGEMENT FOR
TECHNICAL SERVICE FUNCTIONS IN A LIBRARY

TECHNICAL SERVICES OPERATIONS

Library functions like ordering, claiming, receiving, binding, repairing, and so on, can be performed in areas away from the public and could readily be placed in the far back of a lower or upper floor of a library facility. They do require an entrance/exit to the outside for deliveries and lift/elevator access. Technical services functions are represented in Figure 2.3.

READER SPACES

The lack of seating is a common complaint from library users. Poor initial planning sometimes underestimates adequate seating space. Another reason for a shortage of reading space is that, as shelving becomes filled, new stacks are added into areas that once served for reading and studying. Over the years, seating can become so inadequate as to pose a serious problem. College accreditation boards often mandate minimum standards that specify numbers of seating spaces, based on overall primary-user population. To accommodate a variety of users, a mix of seating is the answer. In colleges, students often use libraries for studying between lectures but without the wish to consult library materials at that particular time. There should be a reading area located near the entry. This is convenient and cuts down on traffic within the library. Discussion tables could be in a separate area where talk is not disturbing to others. Some libraries provide enclosed study rooms available for sign-up by user groups.

Users who come to peruse newspapers and new journal arrivals like to do so while sitting in comfortable chairs with low tables for leisurely reading. Although they prefer to be separated from the general reader/study area, they favour ease of access. If there is space, place it within the foyer area. However, this type of seating can be located almost anywhere.

The most serious of library users have come to use the collection. They tend to read with concentration and prefer the seclusion and silence of the back areas of the library where the stacks are located. Quiet reader groupings or individual carrels should be placed well away from heavy traffic.

Seating within areas of special collections are subject to the needs peculiar to the format to be used. Video carrels should be where the video centre is housed, microfiche reader/printer tables should be where the microfiche are stored, map tables for perusing maps should be at cartographic centres. These centres may require some staff assistance but perhaps not quite as much as the reference/computer area, and could be placed almost anywhere they fit into the overall design.

BIBLIOGRAPHIC INSTRUCTION ROOM

Reorganizations are also an opportunity to introduce innovations. At times of cutbacks, support staff are often reduced. Library goals have always been to provide service while allowing for optimum assistance. Optimum assistance can be defined as the one-to-one method of points-of-use-instruction librarians have been using for decades. With the arrival of self-service databases, librarians are in a position to provide a different type of optimum assistance which consists of teaching users how to become self-sufficient. Instruction can take place directly in the library in a closed room, such as the conference room. This room needs to have wiring capable of displaying online resources in a classroom setting for presentations. Telephone access is also required so that the room can double as a meeting place for teleconferences.

COLLECTION DISPLAY

How a collection is displayed and arranged is determined by the layout of the facility. If, for example, there is more than one floor on which to shelve the collection, consider the most expedient way to divide it. What are the parts of the collection that can readily stand on their own? Non-book materials, like videos, tapes, records, films may well be shelved on the first floor, books on the second floor, bound periodicals on the third, archives on the top floor. The divisions should be logical and in large, identifiable blocks so that patrons can remember what the overall arrangement is. If more than one floor is needed for books, divide call-number runs into a consecutive flow, like from A to M, and from N to Z. Prominently display signage that points users to the appropriate stack levels.

TECHNICAL CRITERIA

CODES AND STANDARDS

Codes, standards and guidelines are issued by national, state or local jurisdictions (covered in the UK by the Public Libraries and Museums Act, 1964) to serve as a road map in the design of new facilities. These regulations spring from the powers of the state to protect the public from harm. Regulations may be in the form of regulatory codes or ordinances or may have become law.

Specifications in these documents are largely based on consensus between local law enforcement agencies, national associations for building professionals, fire and safety organizations and insurers. These documents form the basis for calculating allocation of space for collections, readers and staff. They serve as guidelines for technical design criteria such as lighting, heating, ventilating and air conditioning. They provide information on compliance with access for handicapped users and security or safety issues. They offer solutions to noise control. They recommend appropriate signage.

WHO NEEDS TO KNOW

Although the more technical criteria tend to be in the domain of the architectural and engineering professionals, it is up to the librarian to make sure that designers, architects and engineers understand the ways in which standards for libraries differ from other building types and in what manner.

SOURCES OF PERTINENT LITERATURE

Where to find information on codes and standards for libraries? Every regulatory association has standards. Many of these include standards for library facilities. The British and Irish Association of Law Librarians and the American Bar Association, for instance, have guidelines for libraries in law firms. In planning libraries for public use, adherence to official guidelines is mandatory. To cite an example, the Ohio Board of Regents (OBR) sets official OBR Space Planning Guidelines for Public Universities in the State of Ohio.

Guidelines might not be written specifically for libraries but contain useful information for library facilities on heating, ventilating, air filtration and air conditioning (HVAC), specifications for lighting and for floor load capacity. Building specifications are usually governed by laws and local ordinances and information about these can be obtained by calling the appropriate trade organization. Publications in books and trade journals are also good sources to find information on specific library design topics, for instance, Woodson (1992), Ramsey (1992), and Metcalf (1986).

SPACE ALLOCATION GUIDELINES

Standards listed tend to be formula based and take into consideration collection size, staff and recommended number of reader stations.

LIBRARY SHELVING AND FLOOR LOAD CAPACITY

Library shelving is constructed in standard sizes. In the United States, the standard is 36″ long and 8, 10 or 12″ deep. In the UK the standard is set by BS5454:1989 'Storage and Exhibition of Archival Documents'. Shelving weight should be obtained from the manufacturer.

Shelving must have a solid support. Floors constructed for office use are not suitable for library shelving. In the United States, floor capacity for office space is typically assessed to be 50 to 80 pounds per square foot. For library shelving it is 150 pounds per square foot. High-density mobile shelving once loaded will double the floor load requirement. To avoid the considerable expense of strengthening upper floors, compact shelving might best be placed on the ground floor of a building. Manufacturers of this type of shelving will provide floor loading analyses and specifications. A detailed discussion on shelving weight and floor load capacity can be found on pages 89–92 in Cohen (1979).

LIGHTING

Lighting specifications

Lighting specifications are of particular relevance to libraries. The *Illuminating Engineering Society Lighting Handbook*, edited by Kaufman (1987), is a useful source of information. A detailed comparison of incandescent, fluorescent mercury, halide and other types of lighting are found in Cohen (1979).

The architect's recommendations and the project's budget size will determine the type of lighting to be selected. Final choice will take minimum standards into consideration. In the US quantity of brightness is evaluated in terms of foot candles (in the UK, light value is measured in units of lux), a measurement used by professionals to determine light levels. A standard foot candle is equal to the amount of light produced by a plumber's candle at a distance of one foot. For most library browsing areas, the recommended amount of foot candles is 30. For reading areas 100 to 150 foot candles are suggested.

Placement of light sources

The placement of light fixtures is also of significant consequence in libraries. Brightness is reduced once shelves have been loaded. Lighting that runs parallel to stacks causes shadows and makes reading difficult. The best light source is produced from diffused and scattered light. Avoid light that bounces off shiny surfaces. Install grills or panels below a light source and carpeting on the floor. Glare will now be absorbed by the ceiling above and the carpeting below. Because walls tend to absorb light, smaller rooms require more light. Larger rooms require less not only because there are fewer walls to absorb light but also because overhead light spills over from aisle to aisle.

WIRE MANAGEMENT

Planning for suitable sources of power is a must. Installation of equipment, incoming telecommunication lines and phone connections should enter the facility via conduits hidden from view. Lines might run behind walls, the ceiling or a sub floor. Many libraries have columns for added floor/ceiling support. They are also useful for hiding conduits.

POWER REQUIREMENTS

In determining the amount of power that should enter a new facility, more is better than just adequate because adding additional power later on is expensive and funding may not be as readily available. Make a ball park guess on how many computers might be in use within ten years. In the last five years, the number of computer stations in even a small library has tripled.

HVAC REQUIREMENTS

Heating, ventilating, air filtration and air conditioning are important features to consider before the move. This is an area in which the expertise of architectural and/or engineering professionals must be relied upon. The planner has to make sure that all of these aspects have been considered.

HANDICAPPED ACCESS

Many libraries are public facilities. They have to be accessible to persons with impaired mobility, sight or hearing. Specific building guidelines apply for the location and measurements of entrances and exits, stairs, lifts and elevators, rest rooms, water fountains, access to stack collections, study and work desks, photocopiers, computer terminals and media equipment. American With Disabilities (ADA) guidelines can be found in the *Federal Register*. The Architectural and Transportation Compliance Board in Washington, DC provides, upon request, copies of the *ADA Accessibility Guidelines for Building and Facilities*. Foos has adopted ADA guidelines to libraries (1992).

SECURITY AND SAFETY

Security and safety covers fire alarms, alarm systems that secure the premises when the library is closed, electronic surveillance to prevent theft and the installation of sprinkler systems in the stacks to deter fire from spreading. The local fire department will inspect fire alarm systems after the new facility has been opened to the public to make sure they come up to code. A good source to find out about specifications for sprinkler systems or electronic alarms are the manufacturers of such systems.

SIGNAGE

A well-thought-out system of signage should be an integral part of the design plan with funding set aside for this purpose.

Outdoor signage

Above the door to the library the official name of the library should be prominently displayed. If the library has been named in honour of a particular person, the official name of the library should be shown in its entirety above the entrance. A large sign to the side of the entrance and close to the walkway might identify the name of the building to aid the newcomer in locating the place for which he or she has been looking. Appropriate signage nearby showing people how to find the library should be arranged as far as possible.

Indoor signage

Once indoors, the library user should find signage that provides a general overview of the location of books and services. This is especially important for a multi-floor facility. Each floor should have its own layout schematic that shows the arrangement of collections and services. For overhead signage large lettering that is easy to read from a distance should be used. Signage that points the way to photocopiers, computer stations, the catalogue or special collections should be at eye level.

Professional signage

Professionally made signage lends colour and variety to the often somewhat sterile appearance of a library. When choosing a sign manufacturer, look for specific features. Signage should be indestructible and lend itself to a variety of purposes. It should be made in a variety of sizes so that it can be hung from the ceiling, attached to a surface, like the walls or stack faces, or put on desks. It should allow for floor schematics that show the layout of the library and its parts. Particularly welcome is the type that has the 'You are Here' feature. Alpha-numeric signage consists of exchangeable parts. They are useful for layout schematics and signs affixed to book stacks.

If signage is not included in the initial planning and budget estimate, a library ends up having to hand produce its own signage. It is usually made of heavy paper and at times covered with plastic, but often looks amateurish. As many librarians know from experience, home-made signage is often subject to vandalism.

Symbols

Symbols are usually used for prohibitional signage, such as no smoking, eating, and so on. Symbols of this type should be posted at the entrance and be repeated on each floor and on walls.

3

TRAINING AND SELECTING STAFF

The magnitude of the workforce will be determined by the scope of the project.

KEY STAFF

OVERALL PLANNER

One person should be designated to have overall responsibility for planning and executing the project. Most often, this person will be the head librarian. In projects of greater proportions the person in charge might be someone higher up in the hierarchical structure of the company or institution like a facility planner. Selecting the right person to be in charge is crucial to the successful outcome of the enterprise.

What are some of the qualifications the facility planner should bring to the position? One is that the person be able to devote adequate time to preparation and contemplation freed from distractions and different responsibilities for the period of time it takes to see the project through from start to finish. The person in charge must have good communication skills and a background in consensus building between factions inside and outside the library project. An ability to be assertive is an asset. The planner must be a dynamic representative of the library's interests with outside contractors and architects and be capable of safeguarding the functional integrity of the design. The facility planner should be versed in design, cost estimates, bids and contracts, negotiating with dealers and vendors or be someone with a proven adeptness for learning new skills.

Last but not least, the facility planner must be in tune with the library's goals and mission and, in order to learn this intelligence, work closely with the individual whose library is to be remodelled.

HEAD LIBRARIAN

This will be the individual who is most uniquely familiar with the philosophy of the library, knowledgeable about the library's clientele, acquainted with traffic patterns of users and staff, experienced with proper and optimal utilization of collections and services and qualified to formulate a vision for the future direction of the library.

The librarian's primary function is to analyse needs and to capture those findings into a written chronicle. This document, called the Programme Statement, has been outlined in Chapter 1.

Another responsibility of the librarian is to stay abreast of the project's progression. It is essential to stay involved, attend planning meetings, keep informed and remain in the information loop to keep track of developments. During remodelling or construction routine visits are a must.

Most time-consuming, sometimes tedious but always critically important, is the work that has to be undertaken to prepare for the move. Duties and time constraints may require the librarian's whole attention with individual tasks assigned to other library staff.

DISTRIBUTION OF RESPONSIBILITIES

Supervisory responsibilities can be readily divided by task, that is, review of the collection; calculation of present and future collection size; compiling inventories of special formats, equipment and furniture; site preparation; planning and organizing the move; planning the new facility's opening. The librarian should meet regularly with supervisors to keep abreast with the progress of the work and to ensure that those tasks that must precede others are moving along within the timetable.

SUPERVISORS

Team supervisors must have a fundamental knowledge of libraries and their operation. They have to comprehend the intricacies in the order of the subject classification system for books and other library materials. They should be efficient organizers and good communicators who are able to set priorities and accomplish them with little or no supervision and within given time parameters. Supervisors must be able to work in consensus with the librarian, other team members and their staff.

Supervisors need to be instructed about their specific assignments and deadlines. They should be given the freedom to draw up their own schedule of how they plan to get their work done on time and to compile a set of written guidelines for their team. Supervisors should receive some coaching on how to direct and motivate people and the benefits of praise for work well done.

MOVE SUPERVISOR

This position carries responsibilities more unique and weighty than the other supervisory assignments. Organizing and implementing a move is complex and requires special skills.

Qualities to look for in the person entrusted with the move are: experience in human resource utilization and scheduling skills; the ability to understand and work within a construction time schedule; experience in providing accurate time/manpower requirements; dealing with people inside and outside the library's sphere; decision-making in high-pressure situations; an aptitude to be a problem solver.

For complex moving endeavours, assignments for carrying through narrower moving responsibilities may be delegated to coordinators. Coordinators of each sub group would report to the move supervisor as well as participate in the planning of the move.

MOVE COMMITTEE

Many large moves are complicated enough to warrant the convening of a move committee. Such a body would consider all planning and implementation aspects of the move. The committee concept allows for input by knowledgeable individuals from inside as well as outside the library. If the move is to be carried out by a department within the organization rather than an outside company, representation of this department on the committee is necessary.

COMMITTEE CHAIR

A call to meetings, an agenda for the meeting, taking minutes of the discussions, communicating of final decisions to appropriate channels lies with the person who is elected committee chair. Decisions made by the move committee should be documented in writing to maintain an official record of the proceedings. The minutes can form the basis for progress reports.

TEMPORARY STAFF

Although the important players in this undertaking will be the librarian and his or her staff, temporary help may be engaged particularly with the move itself which is labour-intensive and requires many hands for packing and eyes for supervising.

HIRED STAFF

Draw up a written job description that details particular requirements. Temporary staff for the move will have to be able to lift and handle heavy objects. Loaded book carts weigh about 500 pounds and may have to be pushed across awkward terrain such as carpeted floors, door jams, elevator or lift openings, and so on. In the interview process, identify those individuals who are more capable of physical labour and those who are less so. This will help in allocating the workforce by task.

VOLUNTEERS

Volunteers need to know what is expected of them. Requirements for physical labour should be publicized. Often colleagues volunteer with moving the collection. Library colleagues are familiar with library classification systems and their overall expertise makes their willingness to help especially advantageous. Drawbacks are that they may be unable to honour their pledge when the time comes because of the demands of their jobs.

TRAINING

Training the workforce is essential. This task will be the duty of the librarian and/or the supervisory staff. Training needs to be given with the project's time schedules in mind. Thus, training for tasks that are preparatory in nature, should be done first while orientation and training related to the move might be more efficiently accomplished closer to the time of the move. That way, the training can be specific and will still be fresh in the mind of the workforce.

Training should address physical safety. Staff have to be instructed on how to lift heavy objects repeatedly without injury to themselves. Give training on medical and security emergencies and how to communicate them.

If the move involves a large number of team workers, one-hour-training sessions might be prepared. The modules might be offered at various time slots to allow everyone to attend at their convenience.

WORK FLOW

The workforce must be instructed that work is to be maintained at a steady pace and within specific time periods. The plan, its preparatory phases and timetable should be outlined. Workers should be aware of how their contribution will fit into the overall scheme of things. They have to know whether the completion of one task may be required before another can begin.

CLASSIFICATION SYSTEM

For those temporary workers and volunteers uninitiated to libraries and their inner workings, training has to include in-depth instruction on the intricacies of the library's classification system. After the initial orientation, applicants should be given a written test to make sure they are proficient with the system.

A word of warning is necessary here. Some people do not readily grasp the intricacies of a particular library classification system. For example, the often complex LC (Library of Congress) classification scheme has more often than not been a stumbling block for library helpers and the reason why librarians had to let these aides go. Individuals who are not good at details of this type should never be assigned to work with collection assignments.

HANDLING BOOKS

Staff and aides must be instructed in the safe handling of books and overall conservation concepts. If the assignment requires putting books in boxes, detailed packing instructions must be given to the staff.

REPORTING STRUCTURE

Staff must have a clear understanding of the reporting structure and methods of communication that are to be used in work assignments for the smooth handling of possible problems. If access to the collection is provided during the move, the move staff must be instructed on this matter. They should know who is allowed access and how to provide it.

IMPACT OF CHANGE

Consideration must be given to train staff for the new facility and prepare for the changes ahead. For a reorganization to work well, it is necessary to consider the impact of change on personnel.

We live in a world of rapid change, change that influences our social and professional lives. Not only are people moving from job to job, but, within the same workplace, people are constantly expected to adapt to changes. The impact of change often has a profound effect. For some people, change is invigorating. They see it as a door to advancement and as a more interesting way to do a job that might have become boring over the years. For others, change poses a threat so profound that they counter it by resisting. This can be a serious problem for a supervisor.

When staff have to adapt to too many changes at the same time anticipate problems. Change produces fear, anxiety, stress. Questions arise about authority, influence and power, doubts about one's competence and doubts about other people's competence, about expectations and clarity. Before the change, staff members went to work, facing a familiar routine. They knew how to cope with the positive as well as the negative aspects of their job. They knew what was expected of them. They relied on established lines of friendship or tolerance within the work group. They worked within a situation of certainty in which outcomes are predictable. After the change, familiar routines and relationships take on an air of risk. How to fit into the new work setting, what role to play with the boss and within the group becomes an overwhelming concern. A once familiar situation has been altered to one of uncertainty in which outcomes have become unpredictable. As a defence mechanism, people build up resistance, even defiance, to change. What can a supervisor do to confront this problem and find a solution to it?

CONFLICT RESOLUTIONS

ESTABLISH TRUST

A way to overcome antagonism is to let staff know that they are an indispensable cog in the wheel. It cannot be a superficial attempt at making the worker feel good but must be based on respect, honesty and trust. People need to be aware and believe that they are an integral part of an organization and contribute positively to the goals and objectives of the place where they work.

SEEK INPUT FROM STAFF

Involve staff in the coming changes and seek their input. If people are asked for counsel and advice it gives them the feeling of being part of what is about to take place. They feel proud that their concerns are heard and heeded. This gives people a sense of ownership.

TRAIN STAFF

Anticipate that staff may feel uneasy and unsure about the new setting. Training sessions should spell out expectations. The supervisor's praise will very effectively reinforce training and take the fear out of change.

TEMPER RESISTANCE

Not every person has the same level of need. Sometimes there may be just one or two individuals who continue to resist change. Meet with each person. Find out the source of their distress. Discuss what is known about the impact of change on people. Make those individuals realize that their feelings are not unique and that many people react in similar ways to change. But point out that it is essential that a way be found for them to get aboard. Allow these individuals the opportunity to suggest how they might be able to overcome this crisis. If the course of action looks reasonable to you, set up a step by step plan to follow through on it. Then continue to meet on a regular basis to observe and discuss progress.

REWARD ACCOMPLISHMENT

The most potent motivator to help people adapt to change and an increase in productivity is a financial reward. In today's economic climate, salary increases have not been as forthcoming as in past times. Yet, people can feel motivated as well if they are able to satisfy the need for self-actualization. People feel fulfilled if they have successfully overcome an obstacle and can feel proud of their achievement. The recognition they consequently receive through an increase in respect and status with their supervisor, their co-workers and library users can be a great source of satisfaction. Today's employees tend to be better educated, better informed and more independent. They look for opportunities to achieve their needs through recognition of individual contributions, feelings of accomplishment, and the potential for growth and development. They need to be able to trust you. Building of trust among persons and groups within an organization and the creation of an open, problem-solving climate is therefore of great importance.

4

PLANNING THE MOVE

Planning for the physical move itself requires as much attention to detail as planning a new facility. Care must be given to the selection of the method of moving that is most appropriate for your situation. Should a removal firm which specializes in library moves be used? Will any commercial mover be sufficient for your needs? Will the move be carried out by library staff and/or other volunteers? Sometimes the library manager will be able to make these decisions based on the needs of the library. Sometimes these decisions are made for the library manager by higher authorities. What questions should one ask of the potential removal firms? What should be considered when budgeting a move? This chapter will attempt to answer these questions and more.

LIBRARY MOVING SERVICES

There are numerous companies that specialize in moving only libraries. Some perform special services above and beyond boxing and moving a collection, such as consulting in the planning process and assistance in developing move specifications. They will help develop a move budget. They will vacuum and fumigate collections. They will develop the shelving layout for the new location as well as do a shelf reading project. They will implement barcode technology. They will do shelving and equipment disassembly and reinstallation. If you are moving a special collection, some firms will bubble-wrap materials and use acid-free separators. They are trained to perform special integration and segregation projects for collections. Some companies will even do reclassification projects.

A word of warning in using the services of a specialized moving company to develop the move specifications. Some libraries must develop specifications for a request for bids. If you want to have a specialized library mover perform your move and not just any commercial mover, your specifications for the mover must be specific for this need for specialization. Be careful not to use your desired mover to consult on developing these specs. They may not be allowed to bid on the move due to inside information.

QUESTIONS TO ASK MOVERS

Whether you are using a specialized library mover or any other commercial mover there are questions that should be asked of those bidding for the job. The answers to these questions should aid in choosing the right removal firm. Be sure to interview and get bids from at least three firms.

FEES

What the removal firm charges for a move and how these rates are determined may be the most important question for many libraries. The timing of your move may affect your rate. If you have chosen to move on a weekend to avoid inconveniencing your library constituents, the charge for your move may be two or three times higher than moving during regular business hours. If you have a very large moving project and you choose to work around the clock with day and evening shifts your charges will reflect this. You will have to decide if the charges for these special considerations are worth the price.

How are these charges to be paid? Sometimes the payment is due immediately upon completion of the job, sometimes as the move progresses partial payment is expected. Be sure that you are able to meet the payment schedule.

TIME ESTIMATES

Establish what the mover estimates for the length of time needed to complete the job. Are all the firms that you are interviewing reasonably close in their estimate? If not, what is the most realistic estimate? Will these estimates meet your needs? During a move, it is best to plan some flexibility into your timeline. The best planned move can go awry and an extra cushion of time can be useful.

REFERENCES

Checking the experience of the removal firm is as important as determining their charges. If you are not looking at removal firms that specialize in library moves, ask the removal firms if they have ever moved a library before. Though they may not specialize in library moves, some may have significant experience in this area. If they have, ask the names of their most recent moves involving libraries and contact these libraries for a reference. Ask the librarians what went wrong and what went right. If you are looking at specialized library movers, get a list of the library moves that they have been involved in recently. Contact these libraries for references.

If your removal firm has never moved a library, it is still important to check their references. Establish the company's reputation for on-time pick-up and delivery; their record for damaging items being moved; their reputation for handling claims for damaged items.

METHODS

When interviewing prospective removal firms, discuss their method for packing the collection. Will carts be used? Will the carts be shrink-wrapped or covered in another fashion to help secure the collection and protect it from the elements? If boxes are to be used, what method of packing will be used to ensure keeping the books in order and protected from damage through shifting in the boxes? Who will be doing the unpacking? If the movers will be unpacking, will they have sufficient training and/or super-vision to get the books back on the shelves in order?

How will the removal firm handle security of the collection and equip-ment while it is being moved? Boxes and carts of items left unattended while waiting for a truck to arrive may be at risk from theft.

Be sure to discuss any special preservation concerns with the removal firm representatives. What precautions are taken in the care of special col-lections? What precautions will be taken for the collection as a whole? In a move in the city of Cincinnati, a box of irreplaceable archival records was accidentally left outside in the rain and snow during a move at the Fernald Uranium Processing Plant. Steps were taken to salvage the damaged records, but careful planning during the move could have prevented this mishap.

Great care must be taken in moving specialized equipment. How will the removal firm handle this? It is recommended that you contact the vendor of the equipment or the holder of the service contracts for the equipment to get advice on moving these items. In some cases, the removal firm may move the equipment, but the service representative may want to disconnect the equipment and then set it up at the new location. If there is an extra cost for this service, this will have to be included in the move budget. Leased equip-ment may also carry special requirements when being moved. Be sure to contact the vendor from whom you are leasing equipment.

INSURANCE

Inquire about the kind of insurance the removal firms carry and establish what is covered by the insurance. Also discuss the method of placing claims for damaged and lost items. Establish the removal firms' record for settlement for damage claims over the past several years.

ANY EXTRAS

Finally, discuss in detail what equipment and supplies the movers will provide and what equipment and supplies the library must provide. Some moving firms will not provide extra security and if this is a necessity, the library will have to cover the cost. The library may also need to provide supervision for the removal firm personnel who are unpacking and reshelving the collection to ensure the collection is in classification number order. The library may need to provide training for the removal firm personnel in the proper handling of the collection.

PACKING METHODS

BOXES

The use of boxes for moving collections is common. Many commercial movers who do not specialize in library moves prefer this method for moving collections. It is preferred because movers are familiar with the use of boxes and boxes are very inexpensive. Unfortunately, there are serious drawbacks to the use of boxes. Boxes must be fully packed in order to keep from collapsing when stacked on top of one another. Boxes will also need to be fully packed to keep books from shifting inside the boxes and becoming damaged. Books are not all equal sizes, so movers will do some sorting by size in order to fill a box. Thus they will not be able to keep the books in order.

Labelling of boxes is also problematic. If boxes are labelled only on one side, this labelling information can be blocked from view depending on how the boxes are stacked. If time is taken to try to label all sides, too much time is lost. The use of boxes to pack a collection is not desirable if the library must provide services during the move. Books placed in boxes are not easily retrievable.

CARTS

Special books carts have been developed for library moves over the last two decades. These book carts are generally larger than ordinary library book carts. They have closed backs and have casters that allow safe movement on and off moving vans.

Book carts allow books to be moved directly from the shelf to the cart in order. This decreases the amount of labour going into the labelling process. Because the carts are on wheels, it is easy to rearrange the carts into classification number order for unloading at the new facility. Books arranged on a book cart are retrievable if the library must continue to provide services during the move.

A word of caution when using book carts. A fully loaded book cart can weigh up to a thousand pounds. Care must be used in moving this heavy load.

Given the choice, carts clearly have more advantages than boxes.

STACK MOVING EQUIPMENT

Highly specialized equipment has been developed for moving ranges of stacks without unloading the shelf and disassembling the shelving. This type of equipment is extraordinarily useful when rearranging free-standing steel shelving to accommodate a new floor plan or installing new carpeting. Some larger institutions that periodically move ranges of stacks due to gradual acquisition of space have invested in their own stack mover.

Stack movers generally consist of long, lifting units on wheels. These are fully adjustable to accommodate various range lengths. Using a series of crossbars, clamping devices and safety chains the lifting unit is attached to your range. Then using a jack or hydraulic lift, the stack-moving device can lift your stack range and you can wheel the range to its new location.

BUDGETING

There are many costs in a move that go beyond the cost of the contract with the removal firm. Some of the costs that should be considered are listed in this section.

○   *Removal firm contract*. Have a clear understanding of what is and what is not included in the removal firm's responsibilities.

○   *Rigger*. A rigger specializes in moving large objects. The services of a rigger will usually not be required in a library move. Question potential movers carefully on the limitations to size and weight of what they can move and if they will provide for the services of a rigger.

○ *Moving supplies.* If the removal firm requires that you pack certain areas and materials, such as materials on top and inside of office desks and tables, you will have to purchase moving supplies. Be aware of exactly what the moving company expects you to pack yourself. Usually standard drawer-type filing cabinets will not have to be emptied for moving, however, lateral files must be emptied. Armed with this knowledge, you can estimate the moving supplies you will need and budget for the necessary cardboard boxes, box tape, tape dispensers, masking tape, packing materials, markers, or even wooden crates.

○ *Extra staffing wages.* Depending on how comprehensive your contract is with the removal company, you may need to budget extra hours of pay for your current staff or for hiring temporary staff. Extra wages for staff members will be needed if they are involved in directing the placement of furniture and equipment during the move, and supervising the packing and subsequent reshelving of the collection beyond the regular staffing hours. The cost of this may be considerable if the move is being done entirely by library staff members.

○ *Special communication equipment.* Establishing lines of communication during the move is very important. If telephone connections are functioning at both the old and new facility and are covered by staff, this may be sufficient. In moves that cover multiple floors or multiple storage locations, regular telephone communication may not be possible. Consider budgeting for cellular phones, two-way radios or even pagers to communicate.

○ *Equipment preparation.* Electrical, plumbing, heating, ventillating and air conditioning equipment will all need preparation before moving. Be sure to budget for service calls.

○ *Reconnection and recalibration.* Electrical, plumbing, heating ventilation and air conditioning equipment will have costs associated with reconnection after the move. Budgeting for the realignment of equipment should be included.

○ *Storage.* If new furniture has a delivery date prior to the occupancy date at the new facility, a storage facility must be arranged and budgeted.

○ *New furniture assembly.* Everyone remembers to budget for new furniture, but the cost of assembly and set up of the new furniture may be overlooked.

○ *Telephone moves.* Telecommunications costs should not be overlooked. Be sure to make arrangements for the timely installation of telephones at the new facility and budget for this cost.

○   *Computer moves.* Budget for the extra costs involved in hiring experts to set up your computer equipment after the move.
○   *Security during the move.* If you feel that the security arrangements provided by your removal firm are insufficient, be sure to budget for this extra cost.
○   *Loss and breakage.* There may be some loss and breakage not covered by the removal firm's insurance. Even if the removal company's insurance will cover this loss or damage, the claims may take considerable time to process. Try to budget some funds to cover the cost of replacing or renting necessary equipment temporarily while waiting for claims settlement.
○   *Contingency.* Some funds should be budgeted for contingency to cover the unforeseen.

DO-IT-YOURSELF MOVE

It is very rare that a library will make a decision to move the entire contents of its library using its own staff members. The liability involved in using untrained library staff to lift heavy furniture and equipment is too great. However, many libraries have undertaken projects using their staff members to move the collection.

If there are sufficient library personnel and equipment to perform the task a do-it-yourself move can be viable. When considering undertaking such a task carefully check the following areas. Will the library be using book carts to move the collection? Book carts are generally preferred over boxing books for a move. Are the book carts that the library owns sufficiently sturdy to be completely filled and moved over uneven terrain? Few libraries will have enough empty book carts on hand to perform a large move. In addition, the book carts that most libraries own are not designed to be moved over anything but even flooring that presents no obstacles. Book carts can be rented from some moving companies. This option could fill the gap in having the necessary number of sturdy book carts to accomplish the move in a reasonable fashion.

Check the entrances and exits of both the old and the new facility. Will library staff be able easily to move filled book carts in and out of both facilities? Do these facilities have dock-high receiving areas to facilitate loading and unloading? The filled book carts may need to be loaded into a moving van. Are the vans equipped with hydraulic lifts or ramps to load the book carts if dock high-exists are not available? Does the library have qualified van drivers?

All of these questions must be answered before undertaking a do-it-yourself move.

5

REVIEWING THE COLLECTION

Numerous tasks should be undertaken to prepare the collection before the move. Moving books that are no longer appropriate to the collection is not cost effective. Some items in the collection may be too brittle to move unprotected. It is not desirable to move an existing insect infestation problem to the new facility. This chapter will cover various recommended reviews.

The thoroughness with which these reviews can be addressed will be dependent on the time given to prepare for the move. It is suggested that the reviews be prioritized to the needs of the library so that the reviews that are most important can be completed before the move.

WEEDING

The expense and labour that is expended in packing, moving and unpacking a collection justifies the time invested in weeding prior to a move. If a weeding project is undertaken, be aware of the workload of those doing the deselecting and on the technical processing staff who must correct the catalogue records.

Weeding projects should be completed *before* measuring the collection. This is very important to remember to ensure the proper fit of the collection to the new shelving arrangement.

The time period preceding a move is very busy for everyone. If your entire institution is moving, everyone will be involved in their own preparations for the event. Even though it might be difficult, it is important to involve all of your constituents in any weeding project.

The goal of the weeding project should be clearly stated. Guidelines for weeding should be established. This information should be shared with library users. The criteria for weeding differ from library to library. If programmes or areas of research have changed, collections in these areas may be marked for deselection. Various formats may no longer be valuable to the collections. Low use or lack of currency are valid criteria for deselection for some collections. Whatever criteria are used, be sure to communicate these to the library's constituents.

In any weeding project it is important to allow the library constituents the opportunity for a final review of the materials to be weeded. You do not want your constituents to be 'surprised' that part of 'their' collection disappeared during the move. The logistics for this final review will vary depending on the type of collection. For many libraries, leaving items marked for weeding in a public access area is not feasible. Library users might move the books or remove the markings which designated the item for weeding. It may be desirable to move the items to a review area. If this is done be sure that all library users involved in the final review have reasonable access to this area for an appropriate period of time.

PRESERVATION

Items that are in disrepair may not withstand the trauma of a move. Unbound periodicals, brittle unbound materials, items with loose covers, items with loose or brittle pages all are at risk in the move process. Training in safe book handling of the movers, staff members or volunteers who will be packing, moving and unpacking the collection is paramount. Unfortunately, this may not be sufficient to preserve some fragile items.

Books that are in disrepair whose value will not be diminished by rebinding should be identified and sent to the bindery prior to the move. The cost of rebinding is easily justified given the high cost of replacing these items after being further damaged by the move.

Brittle books may be wrapped in lig-free (or archival-quality) board for preservation purposes. Lignin is an organic acid found in plant fibres. It is vulnerable to oxidation. The lignin in inexpensive paper is highly acidic and this acid migrates rapidly to any other organic material in contact with it. Manuscripts wrapped in paper or cardboard containing lignin will eventually be seriously damaged by the migration of acid. Wrapping books in lignin free (lig-free) board is recommended for conservation of the materials. See Cunha (1967). If handled properly, books that have been preserved with this method can survive the move process. The lig-free board wrapper is re-usable and will protect the book for years to come.

When undertaking a project with numerous volumes that need preservation enclosures, a more cost effective method might be desirable. Shrink-wrapping has been used at institutions moving large numbers of fragile volumes. Shrink-wrapping provides needed protection and stabilization and results in minimal damage to fragile materials. The Pennsylvania State University Library used shrink-wrapping to protect 47 000 fragile volumes destined for a move to storage.

The shrink-wrap process is simple and inexpensive. Items are placed between the folds of film, the film is sealed with a heat bar, and then the package is shrunk to the precise size of the item using a hand-held heat gun. Proper room ventilation is necessary during the shrink-wrap process. The selection of the film and other equipment for this process is discussed in depth in the article cited in the bibliography at the end of the book (Kellerman, 1993).

Shrink-wrapping is not a replacement for long-term preservation techniques. This is a new process and the long-term effects have not been tested. But its efficacy in protecting materials cheaply for a move is proven.

CLEANING AND FUMIGATING

Time taken to clean and fumigate a collection is worthwhile. Moving a dirty or infested collection into a clean new facility is undesirable. Cleaning a collection is labour intensive. Each book must be handled individually to either vacuum the item, or to dust it. This individual handling of each volume for cleaning may be done simultaneously with other projects such as checking for preservation needs, inventory or reclassification projects. By combining several activities, staff time is used more effectively.

Damage to collections from insects, silverfish, and bookworms is no longer a significant problem in most libraries in temperate climates. However, it remains a problem for libraries in tropical regions. If food is served in a library and housekeeping is not sufficient, cockroaches and mice may be a problem. Mould will develop when high humidity is present. If any signs of these problems are detected in your collection, care must be taken so that the problems do not move with you to the new facility. Flash freezing of books is one method for ridding a collection of unwanted infestations. This method is preferred over the use of toxic chemicals for fumigation.

RECLASSIFICATION

If a reclassification of the collection is planned, or is in progress, completion prior to the move is desirable. The move will be less confusing with the entire collection having the same classification system. It is also desirable to be able to put the collection on the shelves in the new facility and not be faced with major shifting at a later date to accommodate an ongoing re-classification project.

One library that did not have time to complete a reclassification project mapped the placement of their collection into the new classification order. This was done in order to avoid large shifting projects later.

INVENTORY

If an inventory of the collection has not been done in recent years, this could be useful. Whole sections of books on a specific topic may have gone missing over the intervening years since the last inventory. Not only will you identify items that need to be replaced, you may also identify areas where the collection measurement process may have been inaccurate (depending on method used) and more space must be left for replacement book purchases.

Inventories not only offer the opportunity to identify missing books, but provide the opportunity for a careful shelfreading. Getting the collection into classification order prior to the move can be invaluable.

RECALL

Some libraries may attempt to recall all borrowed items prior to the move. This is especially valuable if the library's entire constituency is moving as well. The recall might be done to ensure the safe and secure handling of all library materials during the move process. This places the responsibility for moving the materials in the hands of the library staff who have been trained in the proper handling of library materials. Using the recall process, previously borrowed items that are in need of preservation can be identified and treated before the move as well.

6

CALCULATING COLLECTION SIZE

A precise assessment of current collection size and a reliable estimate for future expansion are key elements in planning space reorganizations. The collection generally will use the major portion of library space. To be aware of overall collection size is essential in working with planners in order to determine proper space allocations, shelving requirements and moving costs, all major budget lines in a cost estimate. The collection is also the most complex part of a library to move. Having an assessment of the collection as a whole as well as of its parts is the key to a prudent disposition of stack space.

This chapter will offer several methodologies for establishing collection size. It will examine the impact of future growth.

RECORDING THE DATA

The information to be collected should be logged in a Space Data Record. Figure 6.1 shows the elements of such a record. To transcribe every title in the Space Data Record would not be practical since collections are moved in blocks not book by book. A possible grouping of blocks is shown in Figure 6.2. The example is based on the Library of Congress Classification System.

ASSESSING COLLECTION SIZE

Once a workable grouping of blocks for a collection has been established, information can be collected and captured in the Space Data Record. The

Logging Data For Stack Space Allocation				
Subject categories	Current requirements in linear measurements	Estimated growth requirements in linear measurements	Total requirements in linear measurements	Stack allotment in linear measurements/ other

FIGURE 6.1   A SPACE DATA RECORD

Library of Congress class range	Description
A–AZ	General works
B–BJ	Philosophy/Psychology
BL–BX	Religion
C–CZ	Aux sciences of history
D–DZ	History: general and old works
E–FZ	History: America
G–GZ	Geography
H–HZ	Social sciences
J–JZ	Political science
K–KC	Law: general
KD–KDK	Law: UK and Ireland
KE–KEZ	Law: Canada
KF–KFS	Law: United States
KG–KX	Law: other jurisdictions
L–LZ	Education
M–MZ	Music
N–NZ	Fine arts
P–PA	Philology and linguistics
PB–PH	Modern European languages
PJ–PM	Asian and African languages
PN	Literature: general
PQ	Literature: romance
PR	Literature: English
PS	Literature: American
PT	Literature: Germanic
PZ	Fiction
Q–QZ	Science
R–RZ	Medicine
S–SZ	Agriculture
T–TZ	Technology
U–UZ	Military science
V–VZ	Naval science
W–WZ	Preclinical science
Z–ZZ	Library science

FIGURE 6.2   COLLECTION BLOCKS IN THE LCCN SYSTEM

process of data collection will begin with an assessment of current collection size.

COUNTING METHODS

Shelf count

Many libraries keep statistics on the size of their collections. If there is no exact figure available and the library relatively small, staff might do an actual count. It is one of the more reliable ways to establish accurate collection size. The count tallies what is on the shelves but not what is in circulation. Add the number of books checked out at the time of the count. The result will be a count in volumes.

Shelf list count

Another method is a shelf list count. A shelf list is a file that replicates the arrangement of books in the order in which they appear on the shelves. The arrangement is usually in classification number (call number) order, such as the US Library of Congress Classification Number (LCCN) system. The classification number, or call number, is a means of identifying a particular item in a collection and is unique to each entry. Multiple copies or sets of volumes for the same entry are commonly listed on the same shelf list card and hence have to be included in the tally or the result will be an underestimate.

Online shelf list count

Online catalogues provide a convenient means to tally holdings. Every title in a library collection is represented by a bibliographic record. Attached to the bibliographic record are item records, that is, copy 1, 2, and so on, or volume 1, 2, and so on. The screen display will show the total number of items per screen. Number of screens multiplied by the number of items results in a total figure for the collection.

Shelf lists are an inventory of library holdings. Hence, the tally includes books on shelves and books checked out at the time of the count.

A word of caution: the count will be reliable only if the shelf list is accurate. The accuracy of a shelf list count, whether online or from cards, depends on the veracity of the shelf list. If no inventory has been taken in many years, the count will result in an overestimate. An inventory of the collection prior to collection count is advisable.

ESTIMATING COLLECTION SIZE

Estimating collection size is another option.

Shelf measurement

Taking yardstick in hand and doing a physical measurement of shelf ranges is a quick and dirty method to estimate collection size. This method is practical when library materials are housed in different-sized shelves or book cases. The result will be the size of the collection in length of measurement rather than in volume count. Physical measurements do not include books checked out, a figure that needs to be added to the total.

If shelves are filled tightly and the collection consists of standard size shelving, measure the size of a typical shelf unit and multiply by the total number of shelf units in a library.

To convert measurements into volumes divide total length of occupied shelf space by the average number of books per shelf. Calculating averages will be discussed presently.

Shelf list measurement

Another shortcut to estimating size is to measure cards in a shelf list to extrapolate a total volume count. The standard is one hundred titles for one inch of shelf list cards. A sampling formula, designed to minimize error, is offered on page 24 of Fraley and Anderson (1985). Once an average has been established, measure the entire shelf list. The total number of inches of shelf list, times the average number of titles per one inch, equals the total collection size. This count will include all materials in the library, including materials checked out at the time of your count.

CALCULATING AVERAGES

For conversion from linear measurement to volume count and vice versa, an average has to be established for the number of books that fit on a standard size library shelf. Count volumes on a sample number of shelves and divide the total by the number of shelves that have been sampled. Divide this figure again by shelf length. In imperial units of measurement, the result comes out to be between 7 and 12 books per linear foot.

ESTIMATING FUTURE GROWTH

With current collection size established, the focus will shift to the next important step in the assessment of stack space, namely future growth. Future growth is difficult to predict. Book prices change, publication output undergoes increases or decreases, library funding allotments vary over the years. Nevertheless, an estimation of growth has to be made so that growth space for future additions can be estimated with some degree of certitude.

Information on expansion rates

A way to determine the rate of expansion for a library is to look at funding disbursements and past purchasing patterns. Annual book expenditures divided by the average price for a book in a given discipline result in a figure for annual growth in terms of volumes. Another method is to peruse publications that furnish information about average prices and scope of annual publication output in different subject areas, like the *Bowker Annual*.

Effect of growth

What is the effect of growth rates on stack occupancy? Let us assume collection growth to be four per cent per year. From the total collection size one can now estimate future size by a compound growth calculation, multiplying each year's figure by a four per cent increase, namely, by the factor 1.04. Calculating collection housing for the future requires taking the growth factor into consideration. The overall growth rate figure lets the planner estimate how long a collection can remain in its quarters before the available shelving space is exhausted.

For example, after five years, the increase would be 22 per cent over the starting collection size and, within 20 years, it is somewhat more than double the original size. In other words, an annual growth of four per cent will *double* the size of a collection within a period of 20 years.

Uniform growth

In some libraries the percentage of growth may be the same in all subject categories. This would come about when growth is controlled by distributing funding equally among categories. In this scenario, all sub categories in a collection would share equally in the allocation for growth space.

Non-uniform growth

Not all library collections, however, grow at a uniform rate. In a library whose purchases mirror publication output in the various subject areas, a considerable variation of growth will occur from one subject category to another. When one category within a collection grows more rapidly over the same number of years than another, this variation, if not considered, will cause a problem with shelving of new materials. Two per cent growth-rate for one category, compounded over a 20-year period, translates into an expansion of growth space of 49 per cent, while a 6 per cent growth rate over the same time period for another category will mean a 220 per cent increase. Obviously, the category that grows by 2 per cent needs less growth space than the category that expands by 6 per cent.

Example   A sample library has a collection of 15 000 volumes. Stack space required to house the current collection is 2143 linear feet (15 000 divided by

7, the average number of books per linear foot in that library). The average growth for the sample library is an overall rate of 4 per cent per year. Let us assume that the sample library houses four subject categories, each requiring a different amount of space for the current collection and each growing at a different rate relative to total growth per annum.

Subject category	Fraction of total current collection	% Growth per year relative to 4% average annual growth per year	% Contribution of total growth
A	f_A = 0.25	8	50
B	f_B = 0.40	2	20
C	f_C = 0.15	4	15
D	f_D = 0.20	3	15
		Total:	100%

FIGURE 6.3   ILLUSTRATION OF NON-UNIFORM COLLECTION GROWTH IN A SAMPLE LIBRARY

Figure 6.3 shows Category **A** as needing 25 per cent of shelf space to house current holdings; its growth is 8 per cent per year compared to the average growth of 4 per cent for the collection as a whole. Therefore, Category **A** will require 50 per cent of the assignable growth space. Category **B** requires 40 per cent of shelf space for current holdings, grows by 2 per cent versus the 4 per cent overall growth and will require 20 per cent of the growth allocation. Category **C** needs 15 per cent of shelf space to house current holdings, grows by 4 per cent and requires 15 per cent of total growth space. Category **D** requires 20 per cent of shelf space for current holding needs, grows at 3 per cent per annum and requires 15 per cent of the space set aside for expansion.

Let us assume that the sample library's new facility has a total of 10 000 linear feet of stack space. The current collection requires 6000 linear feet of space, thus leaving 4000 linear feet for growth. How many linear feet can be assigned to categories **A** to **D**, respectively? Let us assign space according to needs, as follows:

Category **A** requires 25 per cent of 6000 linear feet, or
  1500   linear feet for the current collection
            and 50 per cent of the 4000 linear feet of growth space or
  2000   linear feet
  ————
  3500   total linear feet

Category **B** requires 40% of 6000 linear feet, or
  2400   linear feet for the current collection,
            and 20 per cent of 4000 or
   800   linear feet
  ————
  3200   total linear feet

Category **C** requires 15 per cent of 6000 linear feet, or
   900   linear feet for the current collection
            and 15 per cent of 4000 or
   600   linear feet
  ————
  1500   total linear feet

Category **D** requires 20 per cent of 6000 linear feet, or
  1200   linear feet for the current collection
            and 15 per cent of 4000, or
   600   linear feet
  ————
  1800   total linear feet

To accommodate each category in the sample according to its needs, the following number of shelf units of standard shelving, 3 linear feet wide and 7 tiers high, should be set aside in the new stack area:

    Category **A**: 166.7 shelf units
    Category **B**: 152.4 shelf units
    Category **C**:   71.4 shelf units
    Category **D**:   85.7 shelf units

A real collection is seldom broken down into just four categories. Large libraries may have a rather significant number of subject categories. Each is likely to grow at a different pace. The perceptive planner will factor in growth variance before the collection has been moved. How? Ascertain the total number of books that are customarily added to a collection in one year. Also determine how many books have been added in each of the different subject categories that have been identified as 'blocks' (see Figure 6.2).

Use the number of volumes added to a given subject category as the numerator, divide the numerator by the number of volumes added to the collection as a whole, then multiply the result by 100. The resultant figure will be the relative percentage of annual growth for that subject category. Repeat the calculation for each and every 'block'.

Capture this information in the Space Data Record. The Space Data Record can now be used for allocating space, a process which will be discussed in preparing the new site for the move.

7

INVENTORIES OF OTHER ITEMS

Preparing the collection for its relocation will be the most time-consuming of the preliminary tasks, but other items will be moved as well that need to be inventoried and made ready for the move. This chapter will enumerate some of them. Conclusions can be drawn from the examples cited on how to prepare other types of equipment not mentioned here.

FURNITURE

Funding priorities tend to favour library shelving, furnishing of public access areas, reader spaces, circulation counters, computer work stations and electronic equipment. A list of new furniture and equipment has almost certainly been compiled earlier for inclusion in the Programme Statement, since cost had to be allotted for it as part of the budget proposal.

Sometimes, limited funding makes it mandatory to continue use of existing furniture for office areas that are not open to public view. If used furniture is to be shipped to the new facility, its condition should be evaluated and a list compiled of all items worth moving. The list should enumerate, room by room, desks, chairs, filing cabinets, and so on.

Staff members should be responsible for packing the contents of their work area in boxes supplied for that purpose. Boxes should be appropriately labelled for shipment by the movers. Personal items, however, should be moved by each individual on their own.

SPECIAL EQUIPMENT

Photocopiers, telefacsimile (fax) machines, computers and computer work stations should also be inventoried. Read manuals for each piece of equipment to make sure that correct instructions for transport are being followed. If necessary, instructions should be obtained from the supplier about moving such pieces.

The best way to move electrical and electronic equipment is by a mover who specializes in moving this type of equipment. A separate contract may be necessary for moving special equipment because of the need to disconnect and reconnect equipment properly and because of security issues.

If the move entails disrupting a dedicated terminal line, contact the network representative or utility in advance of the projected moving date to obtain instructions for proper procedures before, during and after the move.

The shipment of fax machines entails disconnecting and reconnecting a phone line. Arrangements with the local phone service supplier may have to be made.

Photocopying equipment is often leased to libraries rather than owned by them. Notify the contract holder of the impending move and ascertain if the owner may prefer to move its own equipment. This will relieve the library of possible liability in case of damages. If the owner tells the library to move the equipment, a waiver should be obtained releasing the library of any liability resulting from damage during the move. Usually equipment of this type is moved at the last moment to minimize the loss of privileges for library clientele.

SPECIAL PURPOSE FURNITURE

Measure and inventory furniture that serves a particular purpose. A typical example might be a card catalogue.

CARD CATALOGUES

Card catalogues are unlikely to be moved with their contents in place because of the sheer weight involved. If the card catalogue has to be moved with contents, make sure that drawers are secured during movement. Otherwise, drawers and cabinets will likely be transported separately. Make a plan of how and when to prepare the catalogue for shipment.

Card catalogue drawers should be numbered and labelled. If they are not already labelled, it is a good idea to do this prior to the move. It will facilitate quick and efficient reassembly after the move.

Remove catalogue drawers in preparation for shipment only after the library is closed to customers.

SHELVES

Library shelving is the most specialized equipment of all. In a new facility, it is advisable to start out with new library shelving.

If you have to move the existing library shelving, the library will have to draw up a separate contract for moving the collection into temporary quarters. Old shelves will have to be disassembled one by one and moved into the new facility. This is an expense that should have been considered in the initial planning phase and be included in the budget proposal as a separate expense.

ODD-SIZED CABINETS

Into the category of special-purpose furniture fall unorthodox sized cabinets that contain non-book materials. Cases must be measured. Evaluate ahead of time if the cases fit through conventional doors, can be transported via staircases or lifts and what the best method is for moving them. If cases can be moved with their contents in place, decide how best to secure drawers to prevent spilling. If the contents have to be removed, do so prior to the move. Obtain sturdy boxes, store the contents and label boxes to facilitate later refiling.

MICROFICHE FILES

Microfiche cases can usually be moved without removing their contents. Individual drawers will have to be securely fastened with tape to keep them from shifting during transport.

MAP CASES

A particularly telling example of a type of special material whose relocation has to be carefully planned is a map collection. Maps are filed in flat cases of unique width. Each flat case contains several flat drawers. The overall dimensions of the map cases are such that they do not fit through doors of conventional size. The solution is to empty map cases of their contents before the move. Remove maps carefully to avoid creasing, tearing, wrinkling or other damage. This should not be a rush job. Store them in containers, such as map tubes or wide boxes, and mark contents on the outside to facilitate later refiling.

If, for some reason, it is decided to transport maps from point A to B without removing them to boxes, individual drawers will have to be pulled from the case. Secure the contents of each drawer with cardbox and cord to prevent shifting and spillage. Keep in mind that the drawers will have to be turned sideways during the move. In the new location, stack drawers flat on top of each other in order of receipt. Then reassemble the cases in their proper order. Drawers filled with maps are very heavy. Make sure that hired help is strong enough to manage the job.

8

PREPARING THE NEW SITE

The goal of a library move is to place every item in its designated place with little or no adjustment after the move has been completed. This chapter will offer a plan of action which achieves this objective.

CONFINE MISTAKES TO THOSE ON PAPER

In plans which are susceptible to trial and error, designers have learned that it is simpler to make mistakes on paper rather than in reality. This common sense wisdom has particular application to the topic of preparing for a library move. Moving a library collection is a mammoth undertaking. Once the move has been completed, misapplication of space will bedevil the librarian for years to come. Hence, it is preferable to make errors during the planning phases when mistakes can easily be corrected on paper.

MAPPING THE FACILITY

Maps are the first type of paper guides that will be created as a requirement for the move. Maps relay a great deal of information in relatively little space. That is why their use is so prevalent in implementing complex jobs. Maps are easily produced from blueprints.

ARCHITECT'S BLUEPRINTS

Blueprints are architectural drawings that are used to plot floor diagrams and depict location and size of areas. Learn how to read blueprints and architectural symbols. In a library project that involves interaction with architects or engineers, it is likely that blueprints of the facility are readily available. Sometimes, the parent institution has access to blueprints even if the librarian has not and is willing to share them.

LAYMAN'S DRAWINGS

In lieu of a professional blueprint, a rough sketch can be drawn by the layman. An architect's ruler, scissors, pencil and graph paper are needed to make an architectural drawing – or, alternatively, a computer. Blueprints need to be drawn to a particular scale which should be inscribed underneath the drawing. Once an outline has been drawn, the location of outside walls, inside wall, doors, windows, supports, staircases, elevators and lifts should be added to the sketch. Within floor areas, the arrangement of service points, reader areas, offices, stacks or any other locations of significance should be indicated. The number of maps required depends on the layout of the facility.

BASIC MAP

A basic design can be manipulated to serve a variety of purposes. Figure 8.1 shows a two-floor facility and provides, at one glance, an overview of the service areas on each floor. Figure 8.2 is a larger version of the same blueprint and depicts the entrance level only. It serves the purpose of identifying locations of service points, reader/study areas, public desks, equipment, and so on. Figure 8.3 demonstrates how a greatly enlarged version of the same basic blueprint can be utilized to outline the sequence of a book stack arrangement. In the illustration LCCN (Library of Congress Classification Numbers) are used.

MAPPING SHELVES

No aspect of the move will be as intricate as the allocation of space for the library collection and its parts. Mapping shelves for book placement might take anywhere from several days to several weeks, depending on the size of the collection and the complexity of its shelf arrangement.

SPACE ALLOCATION GUIDES

Space allocation guidelines are the key for proper book placement. The distribution of a small library collection might need no more than an outline as presented in Figure 8.3. However, paper guides that show greater detail will

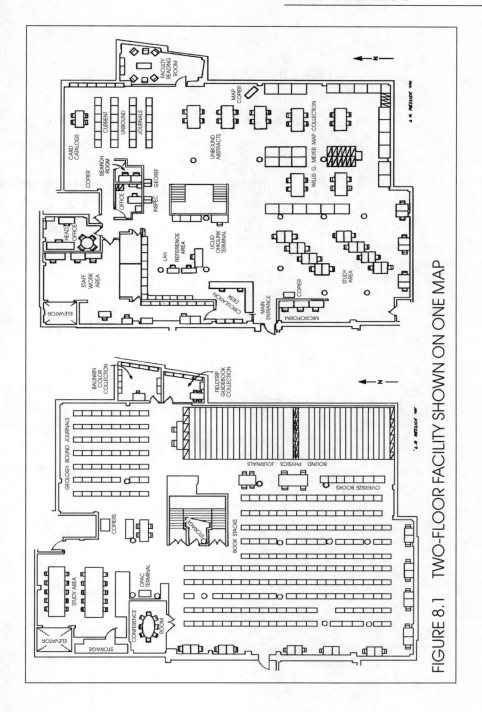

FIGURE 8.1   TWO-FLOOR FACILITY SHOWN ON ONE MAP

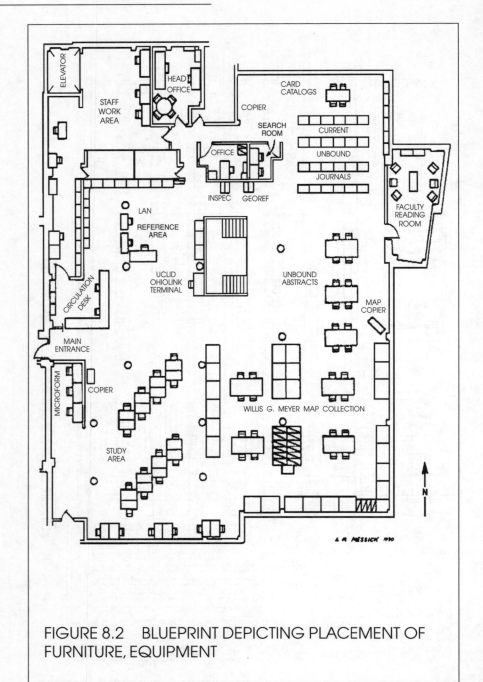

FIGURE 8.2   BLUEPRINT DEPICTING PLACEMENT OF FURNITURE, EQUIPMENT

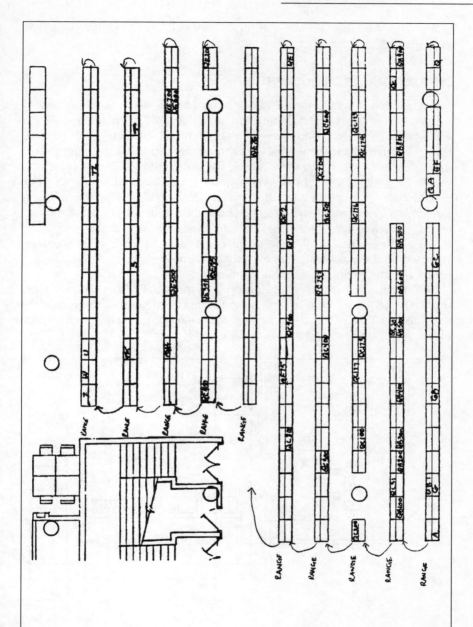

FIGURE 8.3   MAP OF BOOK SHELVES IN LCCN SYSTEM

work better for larger libraries, especially for collections with non-uniform growth rates.

SHELF SCHEMATICS OR WORKSHEETS

The relevance of detailed space allocation guides or 'worksheets' is that they are a replica of the shelving units that are to be used for placement of the collection. They are a front view of a single-faced shelf unit, in schematic form. Drawn to scale, the worksheets should also represent the height of the unit in terms of shelves or tiers. A series of connected shelf units is called a range. Each set of worksheets completed for a range of shelf units can be considered a distinct file identified by its range number. Begin every new range with a new set of worksheets whose label indicates that they belong to that particular range set. This will minimize confusion at the time of the move and eliminate any possible mix-ups. The number of worksheets required for the task will correspond to the number of shelf units and ranges for which space allocations are to be made.

The distribution of space will proceed in the order of consecutive shelf units. The sequence will flow from left to right to the end of the range. On the opposite side of the aisle, the flow will again proceed from left to right like a snake, as illustrated in Figure 8.4.

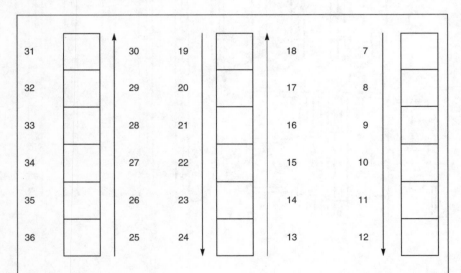

FIGURE 8.4   TOP VIEW OF RANGES DEPICTING LEFT-TO-RIGHT SHELVING METHODS

SPACE DATA RECORD ENTRY

The information which forms the basis for space allocations comes from the data gathered, computed and recorded in the Space Data Records, discussed in Chapter 6 on collection assessment. The Space Data Record contains calculations on current holdings and future expansion. Figures, in linear measurements, should now be transferred to the worksheets. The start and end of each classification number grouping should be written on the sheets according to the 'blocks' of subject categories logged in the Space Data Record. If non-uniform growth has been taken into consideration in earlier calculations, allowances for different growth rates will now show up on paper in the various classification number groupings as either a larger or a lesser growth allotment.

Figure 8.5 provides an example of a completed worksheet. The Figure shows five shelf units. In each shelf unit, the notation indicates 'Begin A–F' ... 'End A–F'; 'Begin G' ... 'End G'. The sample is drawn from a collection using the LCCN classification system and placed on shelves three feet wide and seven tiers high.

	1				2				3				4				5	
Begin A–F	1			8	*End A–F*			7				14						
	2			9	*Begin G*	1		8				15						
	3			10		2		9				16						
	4			11		3		10				17						
	5			12		4		11		*End G*	*Begin GA*							
	6			13		5		12		1								
	7			14		6		13		2								

FIGURE 8.5   EXAMPLE OF A COMPLETED WORKSHEET

VALIDATION FOR ACCURACY

Total number of worksheets represent total stack area. If space allocations, as entered on the worksheets and assigned to the total available stack area, indicate that the collection will fit, the librarian can anticipate moving day with peace of mind.

FLAGGING SHELVES

Flagging of shelves is the next component of site preparation. The purpose of flagging is to expedite the reshelving of books in the ranges of the new facility. Worksheets already show how to shelve the collection from shelf unit to shelf unit and within ranges. This information can now be easily transferred to flags. There should be one flag denoting the beginning and another one the end of a classification category, as shown in Figure 8.5.

Flags should be large enough so that they can be easily read at a glance. Use block letters or lettering by computer. Be brief and concise. Have the flags show essential information to facilitate reshelving for movers and for the staff monitoring for errors. The use of different coloured flags may be useful in certain cases, that is, if books come from more than one location.

A few days prior to the move, flags should be attached to shelves with pressure sensitive tape that can be easily detached once the move has been completed.

FURNITURE AND EQUIPMENT MAPPING

The placement of furniture and equipment should also be mapped out prior to the move. Make a template for every item that is to be moved. Templates should correspond to the scale of the blueprint. By moving templates around the blueprint, plot the position of furniture and equipment to see how well they fit into intended locations.

Once the appropriate placement of the furniture, desks, chairs, equipment, filing cabinets, and so on, has been determined, glue templates into place. Photocopy the result. When the movers arrive with the furniture, use the copied blueprint as a guide for placing the pieces in the facility.

MAPPING UNBOUND JOURNALS

Mapping out the placement of unbound journals in conjunction with the move is another critical task. Journals and magazines tend to be in constant demand by library users. Users expect access to them up to the last minute before the move and again as soon as the new facility opens. A quick and efficient method for transport and refiling needs to be devised.

Unbound issues are best shipped separately and independent from the general move. Shelves for unbound journal issues need to be prepared ahead of the shipment. A convenient way to ease the transfer is to produce index cards for each title. Fix cards to empty shelves with double-sided Scotch tape. No need to worry if issues get mixed up during transport. Refiling will be easy because a place is already set aside for each title. After the move, keep index cards affixed to the shelves. They are a convenient indicator of titles' place during binding or check out.

9

USING SOFTWARE FOR MOVING A JOURNAL COLLECTION

A CASE STUDY: PHYSICS LIBRARY, UNIVERSITY OF CINCINNATI LIBRARIES SYSTEM, USA

The purpose of including the following case study in this book is to promote the concept of computer software as a useful tool for preparing a move. Utilizing software for a journal collection is particularly attractive because the amount of input is clearly definable. Total number of titles received in a library is relatively narrowly constricted while the number of volumes added every year is not. Another factor that makes the creation of a database for journals appealing is the fact that journals have significant non-uniformity of growth. Some titles add one volume over a span of several years while others might add multi-volume sets per annum. This variance in growth has significant impact on the allocation of expansion room.

A further factor making creation of a database compelling in this case study were the logistics in the anticipated move.

THE CHALLENGES

When libraries suffer space problems, storage is often the answer. So it was in the Physics Library, one of several branch libraries in the University of Cincinnati Libraries System. The Physics Library had been in its facility for half a century and outgrown its space. To relieve the overcrowding and make room for new material, parts of the collection were gradually moved into storage sites during the 1970s and 1980s. Most of these sites were not on Campus and hence are referred to as off-site.

In choosing what to send to storage, the decision was made to store periodical holdings. The logistics for storing, marking and retrieving library materials are more expeditious for journals than for books. Choosing certain cut-off years for storing journals provided a convenient bench mark for users and staff to remember which years could be found on the premises and which had to be retrieved from elsewhere. Listings were posted that indicated location for each title and its holdings. Library staff initiated retrieval.

Over time, as the need for storage increased and additional sites were rented for warehousing, many journal titles came to be stored in split runs. A split run is one where the oldest volumes might be stored in one site, the middle years in another, and the most recent ones in a third yet. Adding to this complexity, the physics librarian had also retained in the library proper a few complete runs of titles for which on-site perusal was of the essence. As a consequence, some journal titles had no holdings in storage, others had complete holdings stored in one storage only and the rest was spread as split runs over various storage sites.

When the new facility became a reality, the return of the stored periodical collection was judged to be of high priority. The difficulty of bringing back the physics journals from various storage sites was compounded by the fact that the Physics Library was to be merged with the University's Geology Library. The Geology Library also had periodicals in storage sites, the majority in split runs. A total of 55 000 volumes would have to be shipped from six different locations and merged into one system in the new library facility, a logistical challenge of some magnitude. Making use of the computer for planning and implementing this move was the obvious way to go. We anticipated preparation would consume up to 90 per cent of our time while the move probably would only require 10 per cent, a guesstimate that was borne out.

SYSTEM REQUIREMENTS

The system to be selected would have to be capable of creating a data file for journal titles with linking relationship between data fields and a reporting structure based on linked fields.

The hardware available to us was an IBM compatible with colour monitor and an MS DOS Version 5.1 operating system. As management software the choice fell to DataEase Version 2.5 software, from Software Solutions, Inc. Online menus, shown in Figure 9.1, and the official DataEase manual that comes with the software functioned as aids for developing a data format appropriate to our needs.

```
╔══════════════════════════════════════════╗
║              High Level Menu               ║
║  1. System Administration Functions        ║
║  2. Data Ease Main Menu                     ║
║  3. Backup Database (use drive A:)          ║
║  4. Restore Database (from drive A:)        ║
║  5. Data Entry Menu                         ║
║  6. Reports Menu                            ║
╚══1 to 6══UP══DOWN══RETURN══END══════════════╝
```

```
╔══════════════════════════════════════════╗
║   S Y S T E M   A D M I N I S T R A T I O N║
║  1. Define Users                            ║
║  2. Define Configuration                    ║
║  3. Define Printers                         ║
║  4. Define Screen Styles                    ║
╚══1 to 4══UP══DOWN══RETURN══END══════════════╝
```

```
╔══════════════════════════════════════════╗
║   D A T A E A S E - M A I N   M E N U       ║
║  1. Form Definition and Changes             ║
║  2. Record Entry and Quick Reports          ║
║  3. Full Reports                            ║
║  4. Database Maintenance                    ║
║  5. Database Utilities                      ║
║  6. Menus and Relationships                 ║
║  7. System Administration                   ║
╚══1 to 7══UP══DOWN══RETURN══END══════════════╝
```

```
╔══════════════════════════════════════════╗
║   F O R M S   D E F I N I T I O N   M E N U ║
║  1. Define a form                           ║
║  2. View or modify a form                   ║
║  3. Delete a form                           ║
║  4. Reorganize a Form                       ║
╚══1 to 4══UP══DOWN══RETURN══END══════════════╝
```

FIGURE 9.1   DATAEASE SCREEN MENU DISPLAY

THE PROGRAMMING TEAM

The program was created by a collaborating team. Technical expertise and skill was provided by a computer specialist, Ellen Shostak Rozenson. One of the authors, a physics librarian of many years of experience, provided the professional know-how to advise and guide the programmer in the directions of the project's goal.

PROGRAMMING DETAILS

FORM CREATION

The first step was to define a form for storing the desired information in data-entry fields. Figure 9.2 shows the form that was created. The function of this form was to hold the input data and to display it on the screen. The function keys seen on the bottom of the form, served as operational aids for continued data input, data revision and for report creation. Data needed fell into the following categories:

- type of material, that is, index, journal, continuation
- whether geology or physics (prefix)
- title
- classification number
- publishing frequency per volume and per annum
- summary holdings information

```
serials revised
 1: Abstracts & Indices 2: Journal 3: Continuation 4: Monographic Set    F1MORE
  Classification:                   Active:     Budget:           Prefix:

  Title:

  Call Number:                              Annual Cost: $        .

  Volumes published per year:      .  Frequency of publ.:    per volume

  Summary Holdings:

  Notes:

  Bound Volumes Location:                    Permanent Storage:

  Physical Volumes Added per Year:           Range:        Section:

  Total Physical Volumes:

  Total Linear feet:          .

  Linear Feet Added per Year:      .        Linear Feet Added per 20 Yr.:     .
 F2ENTER F3VIEW F4EXIT F5FORM CLR F6FLD CLR F7DELETE F8MODIFY F9REPORT F10MULTI
```

FIGURE 9.2   DATAEASE DATA ENTRY FORM

○   a note field
           for notations librarians are wont to make, for example
           ceased publication . . .
           changed title to . . .
○   bound volumes location, that is, stacks, storage site
○   permanent storage status
○   physical volumes added per year
○   total physical volumes
○   total linear feet
○   linear feet added per annum
○   linear feet added after x number of years
○   range and section within new stack arrangement.

Information, such as status of a journal title in terms of active or nonactive,
annual subscription cost and source of funding was included in the form as
an added feature, though not essential for the move. A few years later, when
a periodical review and cancellation project were undertaken, this information in relation to specific titles and subjects proved to be of great benefit. It
provided an expedient means of polling library users about frequency of
use and desirability of retaining journal titles.

DATA-ENTRY FIELDS

Unlike manual system categories, online data-entry fields must be defined
precisely. The second step in creating the database considered the type of
information to be stored in the field, how it should be displayed and
entered, and whether it should be limited to a specified range. The process
of filling out the form was to be made faster and more accurate by spelling
out specifications regarding multiple choice fields, calculated fields, table
look-up operations, and default values.

FIELD RELATIONSHIPS

In the third step, relationships had to be defined between the fields that
would serve the purpose of linking all forms together. This step was one of
the more sophisticated phases of building the program.

VALIDITY CHECKS

Each programming step was continuously checked and rechecked. If necessary, changes were made on the spot. Specified conditions had to be met so
that data could be entered properly.

The fourth step in building the database addressed this requirement.
Earlier efforts to define precise data-entry field specifications assured that

the system would check the validity of the information now entered into the fields, made certain that it was the right type of information for the field and that the information entered would fall within a specified range. Moreover, the system would perform all necessary calculations automatically and continually, resulting in a correct, complete and up-to-date information source.

REPORT STRUCTURE

The final step was to define the desired report structure. For each report, records and fields from multiple fields were selected by sorting and grouping on a number of fields and by ordering statistical operations on fields. Then each report had to be formatted, a process that can be likened to a word processor operation. The procedure required definition of print style like page size, margins, pitch and the type style, as well as spatial arrangement for the printout. The reports were given a name and saved in an inventory of reports. To obtain the desired report, the report function key is activated, which brings up a menu from which the user selects the appropriate report and downloads it for printout. Figure 9.3 shows such a report menu.

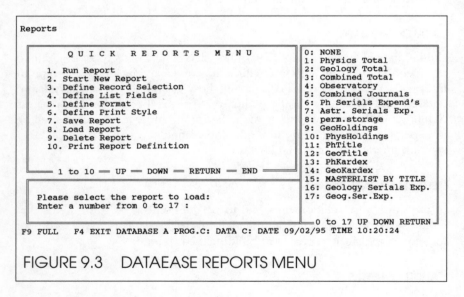

```
Reports

           Q U I C K   R E P O R T S   M E N U      0: NONE
                                                    1: Physics Total
       1. Run Report                                2: Geology Total
       2. Start New Report                          3: Combined Total
       3. Define Record Selection                   4: Observatory
       4. Define List Fields                        5: Combined Journals
       5. Define Format                             6: Ph Serials Expend's
       6. Define Print Style                        7: Astr. Serials Exp.
       7. Save Report                               8: perm.storage
       8. Load Report                               9: GeoHoldings
       9. Delete Report                            10: PhysHoldings
      10. Print Report Definition                  11: PhTitle
                                                   12: GeoTitle
                                                   13: PhKardex
      ═ 1 to 10 ═ UP ═ DOWN ═ RETURN ═ END ═      14: GeoKardex
                                                   15: MASTERLIST BY TITLE
                                                   16: Geology Serials Exp.
       Please select the report to load:           17: Geog.Ser.Exp.
       Enter a number from 0 to 17 :
                                                 ═0 to 17 UP DOWN RETURN ⌐
  F9 FULL    F4 EXIT DATABASE A PROG.C: DATA C: DATE 09/02/95 TIME 10:20:24
```

FIGURE 9.3   DATAEASE REPORTS MENU

EXPLOITING THE DATABASE

Information in the data records could now be sorted and displayed in the form of reports. Ordered by title, the reports provided current collection size

```
                                      MOVING LIST
                                       JOURNALS
      Date:                             PHYS

============================================================================================
                                                                          Total 20 yr
      Call No.      Title                                Location    Bound Volumes    ln/ft  ln/ft
============================================================================================

ph  AS281.D278   Danske Videnskabernes Selskab, Copenhagen. Mat.-fys. skr  Storage    1-3 (1956-1971)      0.55  0.00
ph  AS281.D28    Danske Videnskabernes Selskab, Copenhagen. Mat.-fys. med  Storage    17-9, 21-41 (1939-42, 4.55  0.00
ph  Q1.A63       Archive for History of Exact Sciences                     Storage    1-38 (1960-          4.36  0.00
ph  Q1.A7        Australian Journal of Scientific Research (A)             Storage    3-5 (1950-52)        0.55  0.00
ph  Q1.J6        Studies in Applied Mathematics                           Storage    1-79 (1921-          8.73  3.64
ph  Q1.P5        Philosophical Magazine                                    Storage    s. 6-7; s. 8, 1-36 (19 29.27  0.00
ph  Q1.P5 (A)    Philosophical Magazine (A)                               Storage    37-58 (1978-         6.55  3.64
ph  Q1.P5 (B)    Philosophical Magazine (B)                               Storage    37-58 (1978-         6.18  3.64
ph  Q1.P52       Philosophical Magazine Letters                           Storage    55-58 (1987-         0.73  1.82
ph  Q180.N4A6    Applied Scientific Research                              Storage    16-45 (1966-         4.55  1.82
ph  Q199.J68     Journal of Physical and Chemical Reference Data          Room 405   1-17 (1972-          3.45  3.64
ph  Q2.R43       Recherche, La                                           Storage    7-19 (1976-          4.18  3.64
ph  Q41.L7       Royal Society of London, Notes and Records              Storage    1-41 (1938-          4.00  1.09
ph  Q41.L8       Royal Society of London, Philosophical Transactions     Storage    189-326 (1897-       26.00  7.27
ph  Q41.L82      Royal Society of London, Proceedings (A)                Storage    75-421 (1905-        62.00 10.91
ph  Q46.P33      Annales de l'Institut Henri Poincare                    Storage    1-18 (1930-64)       3.09  0.00
ph  Q46.P33 (A)  Annales de l'Institut Henri Poincare (A)                Storage    1-37 (1964-82)       5.64  0.00
ph  Q46.P332     Annales de l'I.H.P. Physique Theorique                  Storage    38-48 (1983-         2.00  3.00
ph  QA1.I86      Inverse Problems                                        Physics Stacks  1-4 (1985-       1.27  5.45
ph  QA1.U63      US NBS, Journal of Research (B): Mathematical Sciences  Storage    63-80 (1959-76)      1.82  0.00
ph  QA75.5.C627  Computers in Physics                                    Physics Stacks                 0.00  0.00
ph  QB1.A41      Astronomical Journal                                     Storage    71-74 (1966-69)      1.64  0.00
ph  QB1.A41      Astronomical Journal                                     Physics Stacks  75-96 (1970-    10.00 10.91
ph  QB1.A53      Astronomical Society of the Pacific, Publications       Storage    39-81 (1929-69)      7.27  0.00
ph  QB1.A53      Astronomical Society of the Pacific, Publications       Room 405   82-100 (1970-        5.82  5.45
ph  QB1.A6613    Soviet Astronomy                                        Storage    16, 20-30, 31(pp.353-7 3.64  3.64
ph  QB1.A79      Astronomy                                               Physics Stacks  1-16 (1973-      4.18  4.00
```

FIGURE 9.4 EXAMPLE DATAEASE REPORT FOR MOVING A JOURNAL COLLECTION

Date: 7/31/89

```
                         TOTALS FOR SERIALS
                         -------------------
                           PHYSICS/GEOLOGY


                             Active? yes
                             -----------


    .Classification:  Abstracts & Indices

    Number of items in Group:     17      Annual Cost for Group:  $      0.00
    Total Phys. Volumes:       1,141      Physical Volumes Added/yr:    74.20
    Total Linear Feet:         207.2      Linear Feet Added/yr:         12.9



    .Classification:  Journal

    Number of items in Group:    496      Annual Cost for Group:  $      0.00
    Total Phys. Volumes:      16,809      Physical Volumes Added/yr: 1,180.06
    Total Linear Feet:       3,041.8      Linear Feet Added/yr:        202.9



    .Classification:  Continuation

    Number of items in Group:     29      Annual Cost for Group:  $      0.00
    Total Phys. Volumes:         943      Physical Volumes Added/yr:    57.30
    Total Linear Feet:         149.5      Linear Feet Added/yr:          7.5



    .Classification:  Monographic Set

    Number of items in Group:      8      Annual Cost for Group:  $      0.00
    Total Phys. Volumes:         138      Physical Volumes Added/yr:     3.00
    Total Linear Feet:          20.7      Linear Feet Added/yr:          0.3



    .Classification:  Monographic Series

    Number of items in Group:      6      Annual Cost for Group:  $      0.00
    Total Phys. Volumes:           0      Physical Volumes Added/yr:     1.00
    Total Linear Feet:           0.0      Linear Feet Added/yr:          0.1



    .Classification:  Newspaper

    Number of items in Group:      3      Annual Cost for Group:  $      0.00
    Total Phys. Volumes:           0      Physical Volumes Added/yr:     0.00
    Total Linear Feet:           0.0      Linear Feet Added/yr:          0.0
```

FIGURE 9.5   EXAMPLE DATAEASE REPORT FOR
TALLYING TOTAL COLLECTION FIGURES

```
                          Active? no
                          -----------


.Classification:  Abstracts & Indices

Number of items in Group:      19      Annual Cost for Group:  $      0.00
Total Phys. Volumes:          527      Physical Volumes Added/yr:     0.00
Total Linear Feet:             92.4    Linear Feet Added/yr:          0.0


.Classification:  Journal

Number of items in Group:     337      Annual Cost for Group:  $      0.00
Total Phys. Volumes:        7,569      Physical Volumes Added/yr:     1.00
Total Linear Feet:          1,313.2    Linear Feet Added/yr:          0.2


.Classification:  Continuation

Number of items in Group:      30      Annual Cost for Group:  $      0.00
Total Phys. Volumes:          295      Physical Volumes Added/yr:     0.00
Total Linear Feet:             42.1    Linear Feet Added/yr:          0.0


.Classification:  Monographic Set

Number of items in Group:      29      Annual Cost for Group:  $      0.00
Total Phys. Volumes:          198      Physical Volumes Added/yr:     0.00
Total Linear Feet:             28.9    Linear Feet Added/yr:          0.0


.Classification:  Monographic Series

Number of items in Group:       2      Annual Cost for Group:  $      0.00
Total Phys. Volumes:           13      Physical Volumes Added/yr:     0.00
Total Linear Feet:              2.0    Linear Feet Added/yr:          0.0


                          Grand Totals

Total Number of Items:        976      Total Annual Cost:      $      0.00
Total Phys. Volumes:       27,633      Physical Volumes Added/yr:  1,316.56
Feet of Shelf Space:        4,898.0    Linear Feet Added/yr:        223.9
```

FIGURE 9.5   *Concluded*

and annual growth for every item on the list. The enclosed figures show examples of reports culled from the database. Figure 9.4 displays the arrangement of journal titles in LCCN order. Each title indicates site location, volumes in title, linear feet requirement for current collection and growth computed over 20 years. The data is based on an average occupancy of 5.5 volumes per linear foot. Figure 9.5 shows the data arranged by type of material, that is, index, journal, continuation, and so on, and whether or not active, that is, currently received on subscription. It also gives total for the collection as a whole. If the column for 20 year growth in Figure 9.4 shows '0.00 growth', this is an indication that the journal is no longer active. The title still requires space for the current collection but no expansion space.

Figure 9.5 shows tallies first for active ('active: yes') then for inactive ('active: no') titles. The division into abstracts, journals, continuations and so forth was valuable for internal use. The figure is included to give an example of the variety of ways in which a database of this type can be exploited.

The reports took the place of Space Data Records. The data from the reports was transferred to worksheets in a process described in Chapter 8 on preparing the site for the move.

CHARTING THE MOVE

The movers planned to ship library materials by location and not necessarily on the same day. This meant that shipments would arrive from each location separately. Hence, volumes for most journal titles would not arrive in sequence due to the fact that so many titles had been stored in split runs. The new site had to be prepared accordingly. Colour coding was used to facilitate the task. Each storage site was assigned a distinct colour. The movers were told to mark boxes with coloured markers according to our instructions. As library material was boxed for shipment at each location, markers matching the particular site colour were utilized. Boxes were numbered in sequence, rather than by the LCCN system whose intricacies are too difficult for the uninitiated to work with.

Flags were chosen in the same colour as the site colour and then affixed to shelves in preparation for the move. The information on the flags included LCCN notations, title, runs of volumes and years. If a journal title had split runs, that is, had volumes stored in more than one location, each part of the title was assigned a flag in the colour matching that part's location site.

On moving day, movers shelved library materials shipped from the blue site, at one time, materials from the red site at another time and so forth. As movers opened the boxes and reshelved volumes, they looked for matching colours and box number sequence. Library staff supervised the placement of the journal volumes according to instructions on the worksheets, which denoted start and end of titles and their parts. The move and reshelving took place over two days time and required no post-move modifications.

On journal worksheets, the height of the shelf units was changed from the seven-tier system used for books to a height of six tiers only. This was a deliberate choice. Periodical volumes tend to be taller and hence require greater shelf height than books. Library metal shelving allows for height adjustment but, of course, only when shelves are not loaded.

HIGH-DENSITY MOBILE SHELVING

High-density mobile shelving by SpaceSaver Storage Systems Corporation of Mississauga, Ontario, Canada (416 671–0391), was used to house the periodical collection. This type of shelving is also called compact shelving and its pros and cons will be discussed later on in Chapter 13 on shelving options.

The SpaceSaver System sits on solid ground on the lower floor of the facility. The size of system purchased provides a total of 6480 linear feet of shelving, of which 2930 linear feet was needed for the current collection. Growth space is estimated to be enough for 20 years.

A push-button electric system has a safety floor and safety sweep to protect users. The system features a safety lock in each control wheel that keeps the carriages locked in place when someone is using an aisle. Installed in 1989, the system has been found to be safe and surprisingly free of operating problems.

Three stationary shelves anchor the system, one attached to a wall, the other, at the opposite end of the stack unit, is free-standing. A third stationary shelf, located in the middle, stabilizes the system. The total number of carriages is 64. Looking at the stationary shelf at the unit's centre, there are 32 carriages at either side of the centre shelf with one aisle that opens on each side. Two aisles on either side could have been an option but it would have come at the expense of shelf space. This might have been necessary for books but, since the shelves hold journal volumes, heavy simultaneous use was not anticipated. As it turned out there is little browsing of volumes by people standing between the aisles because the system is somewhat intimidating. Three large tables with chairs were placed adjacent to the compact shelves for users, and their heavy use shows that having tables next to mobile shelf units is a must.

Although the SpaceSaver's initial cost ($130 000 in 1989) was considerable, the system provides twice the storage capacity within the same floor area and growth space for 20 years.

TIMETABLE

Formulating the program for the database, entering the data and incorporating the information produced by the reports for preparing the move was time-consuming. It took one computer specialist, the librarian and two assistants two summer months to complete the task.

AFTERTHOUGHTS

Several years after the move, the database is still used to generate a catalogue or inventory of journal subscriptions complete with up-to-date holdings listings. These lists have become a valued part of the promotional material handed out to new and existing library users.

10

ORGANIZING MOVING DAY

CLOSING

To close or not to close during a move has always posed a dilemma for librarians. Librarians are service oriented and the idea of inconveniencing library users is anathema to them. But the reality is that a complete shut-down of library access is preferable as it allows for a swift and focused execution of the move.

WHEN TO MOVE

If closing is the option chosen, what would be a good time to move? Issues for consideration are: When will library users be least inconvenienced? What would be a good season to move a collection?

Preferred times for a move are times of low usage. Times of low usage might be periods when educational institutions and their programmes are not in session, like during the summer or at intersessions. A good season to move is summer or autumn. Inopportune times are winter or rainy seasons because of the unsuitability or uncertainty of the weather. If books have to be moved through the open air, select the season in which a move would pose least harm to the library material.

ALTERNATIVE ACCESS

Not every library has the luxury of being able to shut down all access to the collection at any time. If alternative solutions are chosen, their arrangement should be publicized well ahead of, as well as at the time of, the move.

Where an identifiable grouping of materials, for example, lecture notes, examination papers and the like, have to be made available, arrangements can be made with another library or the departmental office for keeping these materials to hand for the duration.

If only reader/study space is asked for, it may be possible to find a quiet place for study in a nearby library or available classroom or office space.

ACCESS WITHOUT CLOSING

If the requirement calls for access to part of the collection during the move itself, arrangements will require a bit more foresight.

The provisional plan should accommodate only the most critical of needs. These might include access to a narrowly defined group of books and journals, a limited number of computer access stations and some services, such as photocopying. Interim services should be set up in the old site rather than the new one. A library aide should be placed at a desk within a restricted area while the bulk of the move takes place elsewhere in the facility. It should be possible to reach the aide by telephone. Once the new facility is ready to provide services in its new quarters, the interim access point should be eliminated.

The most inconvenient case is when it is virtually impossible to say what part of a collection must be accessible. An example might be a law library where lawyers or students require access to statutes or briefs for court cases. It might be necessary to keep significant parts of the collection behind to be moved later on. Such a case will require meticulous site preparation prior to the move since space will have to be left open in the new facility to be filled later with the rest.

BOOK RETURNS

Most libraries have an arrangement that allows users to return books without entering the library itself. During the move, returned books should be accumulated in boxes and their return registered only after completion of the move.

A problem might arise if users were to return large numbers of books on the library's moving day. This might readily occur if the entire college or research facility was to be moved at the same time as the library itself. Users need to be forewarned that such late returns are not welcome. Users need to be given the date of the move ahead of time and informed of the dates during which library materials may or may not be returned.

GIFT ACCEPTANCE

Gifts received through the mail can be put aside until a later date. In the case where libraries and colleges or departments move at the same time, users might want to donate gifts to the library on moving day so that they do not have to transport them to their own new offices. Publicize when gifts will be accepted and when not. An option is to box up gifts and keep them in a storage room until normal operations resume.

CHANGE OF ADDRESS

Make sure that address changes have been taken care of. A change of address may require several weeks for the notification to go into effect. Publishers, vendors, suppliers and the post office need to be aware of the change in the library's mailing status.

PUBLICIZING THE MOVE

The parent institution must be kept abreast of any interruptions in library services and any alternative plans for library users to access library materials during the move. One notice will not suffice. A rigorous public relations campaign should be undertaken ahead of the action.

Many organizations have in place formal publication channels through which changes, such as a library move, can be announced. At colleges, faculty announcements, student newspapers or an electronic bulletin board might be a good way to publicize the move. Posting printed notices on regular campus bulletin boards and in student residences works well. In smaller library settings where the total number of primary users is finite, the courtesy of individual letters sent out to inform users of the impending changes may be appropriate.

SIGNAGE

No matter how many notices are placed, there are bound to be people who will have missed the announcement. Signage might be a good way to fill this gap. Attractive, eye-catching signs should be placed in and around the library announcing the coming of the move, its date and other pertinent information.

Signage is also an important aspect of communication during the move itself. If the library closes during the move, but has arranged for an alternate site to provide access to services and resources, display this intelligence with signage.

THE MOVE PLAN

Once the preliminary move considerations have been taken care of, the time has come to draw up a move plan. A detailed plan needs to be in place and daily work routines for the workforce should be established. They must specify the line-up of workers, work hours, break times and meal breaks. Work schedules are to be communicated to workers and to all support personnel. Plans must include provisions for steps to take in case of a medical emergency or accident.

LOCATIONAL ASSIGNMENTS

Each aide should be assigned the responsibility for a specific work location and spot. Individuals must be informed of the importance of maintaining their assigned station even during lulls in the action and must agree to this arrangement. Only persons assigned as 'rovers' may be free to roam between sites. They are the runners that keep up with communications. They are to provide assistance to aides stationed at assigned locations and to the moving crew as it migrates from the old to the new facility.

The assigned locations might be as follows: at the old site to oversee unshelving and loading of books trucks, at the old site's receiving dock where carts are to be wheeled into departing vehicles, at the new site's receiving dock and at multiple points within the new library to oversee unloading and shelving. Other locations might be determined according to circumstances. Each aide should be provided with blueprints of the moving plans.

CODING

In a large move where individuals may not know each other well enough to recognize that they are part of the same team, special badges or the same brightly coloured caps could serve to identify moving team members. Coloured overalls or shirts can be worn to help identify supervisors and others.

COMMUNICATION

Decisions may have to be conveyed speedily during the move and means of communications have to be planned for. Communication activities surrounding the move must be both internal and external. All library personnel must remain fully informed of the move schedule, procedures, timetable and other pertinent information and know what to do if a problem arises. If access to a part of the collection is provided during the move because of necessity the move staff must be instructed in this matter. They should know who is allowed access and to where.

The physical method of communicating between members of the move team at the time of the move must be carefully thought through. It is highly desirable that phones in the old facility are still operable during the move and that the ones in the new facility are already in service, as well as cellular phones or pagers if required. Runners are an option as well.

WHAT NOT TO DO

Movers should not be made to follow written instructions and to interpret moving directions while the move goes on. The purpose of the move plan and the site preparation prior to the move is to assign to movers the heavy labour of loading and unloading, unshelving and reshelving with the move team to oversee that the plans are followed precisely.

UNLOADING AND SHELVING

The final phase of the move is the unloading and shelving of materials as they arrive in the new facility. It is at the new facility where most of the library aides will be needed to oversee that books and journal volumes are shelved accurately and with dispatch. Their task will be guided by work-sheets created for site preparation and completed with data during the preparatory phases. These are the definitive guides for book placement.

11

OPENING THE NEW FACILITY

An endeavour that encompassed planning and moving a library into an attractive and expanded setting has been completed. The time has come to tie up loose ends.

FINAL INSPECTION

During the construction and installation phases of the project the astute facility planner would have made routine inspections as a quality check to guarantee that all provisions of the Programme Statement are being followed according to contractual agreements.

Now that the library has been occupied, a final re-examination of all construction and installation features is in order to make sure they have been done according to plan. It is wise to actually try out installations and equipment. The inspection should include carpeting, lighting, signage as well as telephones, fax machines, security and alarm systems, the theft-detection system and any electrically wired systems, such as photocopiers.

LIST OF OUTSTANDING ITEMS

Compile a list of items that documents everything that is not up to specifications and should be completed before final payment is made to the contractor, architect, moving company or any other business firm.

FINAL COLLECTION ADJUSTMENTS

An inspection of book stacks and of the arrangement of the collection should also be undertaken. In theory, there should be little or no need for changes if site preparation was precise and the move carried out according to instructions. In practice, however, minor modifications are inevitable. There will be gaps between sets of books that need to be closed, such as at the start and end of individual book groupings and other similar adjustments.

Even in a well-ordered move, books are placed on shelves without regard to neatness. On opening day, stacks should look immaculate and well-ordered.

After the inconvenience of the closure and the flood of publicity, expectations will be high that the collection not only looks well-organized and uncluttered, but that individual items are readily located. A last-minute shelf reading review is recommended to ascertain that books have been shelved accurately within their classification order and filing errors are corrected.

PUBLIC RELATIONS

People will want to use the library right away, partly because it had been closed and partly out of curiosity.

Prior to opening, have a staff member brainstorm and prepare documentation and promotional leaflets as public relations tools. Employ an art or design student or a local studio to come up with an appropriate yet eye-catching design. Have maps drafted to depict layouts and stack arrangements on the various floors. Communicate open hours. Emphasize new features, new services, new equipment.

Place handouts on tables at the entrance and into the hands of your staff for distribution to those who come to visit the new facility when it opens.

Notify the public that the library has once again opened its door. Use this opportunity to promote the library and to increase local awareness of its existence and excellence.

If new policies are to be introduced, it is appropriate to institute these changes upon opening in new quarters.

CELEBRATING

The successful conclusion of a move calls for a round of celebrations.

STAFF APPRECIATION

Treat the circle of staff which has been most closely associated with the project. A party, a slap-up lunch or a picnic with champagne and strawberries will help make the event a memorable one. Use this opportunity to tell staff how much their effort and hard work is appreciated. Let them know that it was due, in no small way, to their cooperation and participation that the new facility has become a reality. A celebration like this is a unifying experience and will do much to assuage the feeling of deflation often associated with the completion of a difficult undertaking.

RECOGNITION CEREMONIES

A special ceremony should be held for all people from inside and outside the library who participated in the project. Invite those who have been involved with planning operations, those who have volunteered their time with the move, those whom you have hired and others whose efforts should be acknowledged. This is an opportunity to thank individuals and groups for their special contributions. Recognition awards might be given out as a token of appreciation.

OPEN HOUSE

For the public at large, an open house event with refreshments is the ideal way to show off the new library. Light refreshment might be served. Tours and publicity handouts should be offered. Library staff and volunteers should be at hand to take people around to introduce the facility and answer questions about new arrangements and innovations. Capitalize on what has been accomplished.

DEDICATION

A formal dedication is often envisioned when a large or prestigious library has moved into new quarters. An event on a grander scale requires planning and preparation. A committee might be formed to make plans about the type of reception to have and the people to be invited.

PART TWO

ALTERNATIVES TO A NEW LIBRARY FACILITY

In today's economic climate, new space may not be forthcoming and alternatives to a new construction may have to explored.

Part Two of this guide looks at alternatives to space problems that can be used when a new or renovated facility is not within reach, and explore solutions that have been found to be viable answers to libraries' space problems.

A common practice is to make more economical use of existing space. Shelving is added to the existing space or additional room(s) are allocated by the academic department whose clientele the libraries serve. Such a situation calls for a partial or sectional move of the collection, a topic to be explored later.

Increasing the density of space by various shelving options is another solution. Compact shelving, for one, is not a recent innovation but its high initial cost has often been the reason why institutions have shunned away from acquiring it. In the long run, however, compact or high density shelving is obviously more affordable when compared to construction outlays. It provides significantly more expansion space over the years than standard shelving. Compact shelving and other shelving options are explored in Chapter 13.

The practice of storing library materials in remote facilities situated on less costly sites has found acceptance of late. Storage facilities of this type are often shared by several institutions in a region. Chapter 14 illustrates the concept of regional depositories and describes one such model in some detail.

Other alternatives that libraries can consider are the conversion of printed materials to different formats and the exploration of the concept of access versus ownership, where library consortia share their collections and a document delivery agreement. The pros and cons of this idea are considered in Chapter 15.

Alternative solutions need to be as carefully evaluated and planned as any other library project with long-term consequences. The decision should be based on an assessment of goals and with an awareness of the impact of these goals on future space, collections and services.

12

IN-HOUSE SHIFTING

SECTIONAL MOVES

In many libraries stack management becomes unwieldy over the years. One area of shelving might be severely overcrowded while another is only sparsely occupied or even empty. Most often, the cause for this can be found in the past when space was allocated with insufficient foresight. But there might be other reasons. The acquisition's commitment might have become smaller in one subject field but increased in another because of changes in the interests of library constituents or due to fluctuations in publishing output.

A situation like this calls for a sectional move. Shifting sections of collections or shelves within sections will result in a more equitable distribution of available space. Overcrowding will be eased and books can be added again in previously congested areas.

PLANNING BEFORE SHIFTING

In a sectional moving project, the difficulty is not lack of space but that space is just not where it is needed. It is a fallacy to assume that modest shifts do not need advance preparation. Nothing could be further from the truth. Shifting is a move like any other and will work out better in the long run when it is based on thoughtful planning.

ASSESSING SPACE REQUIREMENTS

Determine total shelf space available and shelf space occupied by the current collection. The balance is space available for redistribution.

GROWTH VARIATIONS

An assessment of differential growth for the various categories in the classification system is advisable. The fact that some sections of the collection have outgrown their originally allotted growth space more quickly than others is an indication that there is a pattern of non-uniform growth. Just by looking at the collection, it will be obvious which sections have grown more than others but the individual variances within classification number groupings may not be as readily apparent. Looking at past purchasing patterns might prove to be a more reliable method of quantifying variations in growth rates. A technique for computing non-uniform growth is discussed in Chapter 6 on calculating collection size.

LOGGING DATA

Space computations should be retained in a Space Data Record, a concept introduced in earlier chapters. When compiling the data, differentiate between sub categories in the collection that are representative of the congestion problem. For each grouping, compute characteristic growth rate. Figures should be in linear measurements. Keep in the Space Data Record the inventory of space for current needs and space to be allotted for expansion.

FLAGGING SHELVES

The information in the Space Data Record is to be transferred to flags. Flagging of shelves to prepare for a move is discussed in Chapter 7 on site preparation.

Prior to shifting, attach flags to the shelves to indicate where a particular classification number grouping is to start and where it is to end. Differentiate between the space needed for current holdings and that for expansion by using colour coding. For example, blue-coloured flags could be used to demarcate space for current holdings and yellow-coloured flags to symbolize the space that is to be left vacant.

SECTIONAL SHIFTING

Shifting without freeing shelves of books can be accomplished if it is done from back to front. Flag notations have to be followed carefully. Shifting will advance in reverse order from sub category to sub category, with blue flags indicating space for books and yellow flags space for expansion.

Start at the end of the stacks rather than the front. Leave open the expansion space for the last classification number segment, as indicated by the yellow flag. Place books on shelves in the place set aside by the blue flag. Repeat this process for every sub category in reverse call number sequence. As shifting progresses, space begins to be created between the categories. Books may still have to be put on trucks or set in the aisles but only minimally. When the shifting is done, books will have been reshelved as indicated by the flags.

Boxing books and storing them until space allocation and flagging has been completed is an alternative that can be pursued as well. It will allow the librarian to work with empty stacks and to move books back to the shelves front to back in an order that is more easily followed than reverse shelving.

PARTIAL MOVES

Sometimes overcrowding has become so absolute that there is no room left for loosening the collection. New books can no longer be shelved, journal volumes returned from binding can not be added to journal runs. A common solution to this predicament is to squeeze a couple of shelves into the existing library configuration. The result is that sections of books have to be rearranged at a cost of much labour in an effort that, by all estimation, is going to be short-lived at best.

ANALYSING GAINS OR LOSSES

Before repeating this pretense of a solution year after year, the impact of growth on space should be analysed. An example illustrates the point.

A sample library has a collection of 15 000 volumes. Space for shelving the current holdings is 2143 linear feet, based on an average shelving capacity of seven books per linear foot. Annual rate of growth is four per cent.

If the library were to add four shelf units of standard size, each measuring 3 linear feet in width × 7 tiers high, the gain of space will 84 linear feet. The sample library is said to grow at the overall rate of four per cent per year, or 85.7 linear feet. As can readily be seen, the addition of four shelf units is equal to one year's growth in the sample library. To undertake the laborious task of reshelving for the gain of one year is inefficient.

The result of having analysed the problem is that instead of adopting a gain that is so short-lived as to be impractical, other solutions might be proposed and taken into consideration. Viable alternatives to solve a space problem are presented in the following chapter.

SATELLITE RESOURCE CENTRES

Sometimes the parent organization makes available an additional room or two to help solve a space problem. Rather than use the additional space to string out the collection over a series of rooms, especially unconnected ones, a bit of resourcefulness is in order to make more imaginative use of the newfound areas.

For example, one room might serve as an electronic information centre. This room would have to be adjacent to where library staff are situated so that reference assistance is available. Another solution might be to single out a part of the collection that can be separated from the rest. Possible candidates might be bound journals, dissertations, multimedia or map collections. Combinations that fit together well by context are unbound journals and newspapers; popular materials/best sellers and new books; technical reports and government documents; conference proceedings and society publications; rare and archival material.

How to best utilize additional space in an innovative manner will depend on the type of library and its clientele. With ingenuity a space can be turned into a place that will please library clientele while, at the same time, provide space relief.

13

SHELVING OPTIONS

COMPACT SHELVING

Increasing the density of space by compact shelving is an effective alternative to relieve overcrowding in a library. Invented and patented by the Swiss engineer Hans Ingold in 1947, the system was originally marketed under the name COMPACTUS because it compacts book shelves by eliminating aisles between them.

Before librarians can decide whether such a system is a viable option for them, a basic understanding of what movable compact shelving is and how it functions is required. Compact shelving is a special type of storage equipment that significantly increases the capacity of library storage space.

HIGH-DENSITY MOBILE SHELVING

There are various types of compact shelving. The one that has become the most often used system in libraries is the high-density mobile storage shelving that is mounted on platforms that are sunk into a sub-floor. Anchored into the platform are steel frames which support wheeled carriages that move laterally on tracks. A typical carriage is 88 inches high and features double-sided, 3-foot wide standard library shelving, placed back-to-back. Each carriage can be anywhere from two to six shelf units deep.

EQUIPMENT STABILITY

Stability is provided by stationary shelves placed at either end of the system. Depending on the overall length of the system or number of carriages, one or more stationary shelves are placed in-between the end shelves for greater stability. The face of every range is covered by a side panel which can be finished to specifications in wood panelling or metal finish. At the turn of a mechanical handle or at the push of an electronic button, attached to the side panel, the carriages move sideways to create an opening between the mobile book shelves.

SAFETY DEVICES

Safety devices protect users from injury that may be caused by the closing of an aisle while it is occupied. It is essential that the carriage is not activated while somebody is inside an aisle to prevent a user from being sandwiched between ranges. A safety device in the floor, that is activated by a weight of 25 pounds, stops all carriage movement whenever a person enters an aisle. A safety sweep attached to the bottom shelf acts as a brake if it senses an object lying on the floor. For electrical systems, a red indicator light on the push button panel shows that a person has entered an aisle. When not in use, the indicator light is green. For propelling one or two ranges at a time, the manual system works surprisingly smoothly and easily. Electrical systems work best for units consisting of many ranges that would be too heavy to move manually.

FLOOR LOAD CAPACITY

A possible drawback of compact shelving is its considerable weight. Whereas ordinary shelving requires a floor load capacity of 100 to 150 pounds per square foot, compact shelving will require up to 287 pounds per square foot. If compact shelving is considered, floor load capacity has to be ensured to make certain that the floor is capable of bearing the heavy weight of the steel installation.

LIGHTING REQUIREMENTS

The arrangement of lighting fixtures above the moving stacks is also some-thing to plan beforehand. Regular ceiling lighting will not suffice. Once shelves are loaded with books, brightness is diminished considerably. Also, as carriages move back and forth, light does not fall directly into the open aisle. Newer compact systems have light fixtures attached to the carriages, an innovation well worth the additional cost.

BENEFITS OF USE

By eliminating aisles, compact shelving provides 100 per cent more storage within the original floor area, thereby doubling storage capacity. It also frees up expensive floor space area that can be used for other purposes. For collections that receive limited simultaneous use, compact shelving is an ideal solution to provide growth capabilities over many years.

COST

As pointed out in the case study, the initial installation of a compact shelving system tends to be expensive yet its potential for storage and growth make it cost-effective in the long run.

OTHER SHELVING

Librarians are very resourceful and have found means of making maximum use with limited shelving space. The following types of shelving options have been used successfully in libraries to make denser use of library space and thus their collections.

DOUBLE SHELVING

Double shelving of books can be done if the library already has very deep shelving that is not fully utilized. If this arrangement is used, labelling of the shelves must be done with care. Training of shelvers is equally important so that the consecutive order of the shelving arrangement stays intact. Shelf reading of shelves must be done frequently to ensure that books are in their correct place since the spine of the books shelved in the inner row is not visible to the retriever. Double shelving works best for lower-use items, such as back runs of bound journals or for archival materials.

SHELVING BY SIZE

Shelving by size is an option used at library facilities where shelving is not open to the public and materials are retrieved exclusively by staff.

The advantage of shelving by size is that it makes fullest use of available shelf space.

The disadvantage of this type of shelving is that library users can no longer browse the collection, that materials are not shelved within subjects in roughly the order of publication date, that a well-working system of guides needs to be developed, or barcoding introduced so that book retrieval is less of a nightmare for the library personnel responsible for retrieval and reshelving. There are also costs involved for initial reshifting, relabelling of books and records and signage and flyers for staff and the public.

Shelving by size is most often used for storage facilities, a topic explored in the following chapter.

14

STORAGE OPTIONS

OFF-SITE STORAGE

Storage is a consideration for books that are used infrequently yet judged worth keeping. Large, older libraries find that storing is a more politically tenable option than a massive weeding project.

Whether the off-site storage is a closet down the hall from the library, a storage area in another building or a remote warehouse, care must be taken in the selection and preparation of items that will go into storage. Careful consideration should be devoted to planning the logistics for identifying and retrieving items from storage. It is important to remember that if an item is worth keeping it must remain accessible.

COMMUNICATING GOALS

There will be less resistance to putting parts of the collection into storage if users and library personnel are in agreement with the goals of the project. When undertaking a project of this type, members of different constituencies affected by this undertaking must be consulted. All constituents need to understand the benefits of such a move. The goals of the new arrangement must be clearly stated. If the goal is to relegate parts of the collection to storage in order to provide more space for specific needs, such as electronic resources, more reader space, or stack space for newer materials, everyone must be made aware of these objectives. Clientele should be made aware of what type of access to stored materials they can expect and within what time period.

STORAGE CRITERIA

The actual selection of items or groups of items to be stored should be based on standards that have been mutually agreed upon. Foremost, all materials must be of permanent educational and research value. Other criteria considered may be circulation history, imprint date, classifications in subjects that are no longer relevant to the library's clientele or books that are 'at risk' because of their size or condition.

FINAL REVIEW PROCESS

Items selected as candidates for storage should be marked with flags or dots. An alternative to these marking systems is the creation of lists. Once items have been identified, librarians and library users who wish to be involved in a final review can make their final pass through the collection and voice their opinions.

CHANGING HOLDING RECORDS

Once the items have been selected for storage, bibliographic records need to be changed in order to reflect the new location. Libraries with online catalogues will find this task more easily accomplished than those with card catalogues. Library suppliers carry transparent plastic covers with the word 'Storage' prominently displayed on top that can be slipped over the card like a sleeve.

PREPARING FOR STORAGE

Preparation for storage is also necessary. Is the storage area secure? Is it dry and at appropriate temperature and humidity for storing the format of materials that will be housed there? Is the floor load capacity sufficient? Is lighting sufficient to support browsing and retrieval? What will be the cost of adapting the proposed storage area to the needs of your library? How much material will fit into the space? For how long will the space serve its purposes? What is the distance to the storage facility and how often will someone have to access it to retrieve material? Will it be necessary to staff the storage area on a daily basis? What will be the frequency and schedule for retrieval from the storage area?

The move of materials destined for storage should follow a planning process similar to that for moving a complete library.

REGIONAL DEPOSITORIES

Regional depositories are increasingly seen as an answer to the problems of space and escalating construction costs. Built on less costly sites and designed primarily to warehouse large numbers of materials, these auxiliary facilities are capable of storing at lower cost permanently held, important but infrequently used library materials. A facility of this type sometimes is shared by more than one institution. Usually built within a radius of 20 miles, the site must be equally accessible to participating members, with the added advantage of shared administrative costs through joint management and shared transportation. It also offers the incentive of eliminating duplicate holding.

EXAMPLE OF A DEPOSITORY FACILITY

The South West Ohio Regional Depository (SWORD) is one of three storage facilities that have been built in the State of Ohio (USA) in recent years. Occupied in September of 1994, SWORD serves the University of Cincinnati, Miami University at Oxford, Ohio, and Wright State University at Dayton, Ohio. The depository was funded by the Ohio Board of Regents in the State of Ohio. According to documented material, the cost of the entire building, including shelving and major equipment, was 2.5 million dollars. The cost per volume stored for library storage space, shelving and major equipment comes to less than $1.75.

Holding capacity

The first module is designed to hold between 1.2 and 1.5 million volumes. Three additional modules are to be added in the near future. The depository contains four rows, 74 sections per row, of 30-foot shelving, or over 18.5 miles of shelving. The shelves are 54 inches by 36 inches. A pneumatic fork-lift is used to hoist workers almost 27 feet into the air for retrieval purposes. The fork-lift retriever features a platform, custom-designed and constructed to slide over the forks. Guide rails along the shelving provide for automatic steering of the fork-lift device.

Shelving method

Library materials are stored by size in trays for individually catalogued volumes, or in boxes, for uncatalogued collections of materials. The manner of shelving has been facilitated by the advent of barcoding. Books are barcoded and so are shelves. A scanner scans barcodes for ready retrieval or reshelving. Barcodes are linked into online records.

Preservation environment

The depository creates an ideal preservation environment for the storage of books. Equipped with a special low intensity, high pressure sodium lighting system, the storage module has a separate HVAC (heating, ventilating, air filtration and air conditioning) system and dehumidifying system with particulate and gas filters, extra insolation and vapour barriers, no roof penetrations, no wall penetrations to the outside from the library storage area, a special dock seal, and specially sealed doors. It is designed to maintain a steady temperature of 58° Fahrenheit in the winter and 65° Fahrenheit in the summer with incremental changes as the seasons change. The relative humidity will remain at 40 per cent in the winter and at 50 per cent in the summer. A state of the art multiplexed fire and security system provides for maximum protection.

Accessibility

Materials are readily accessible to users through OhioLINK, a database that displays library holdings state-wide as well as through the online catalogues of each university whose holdings are stored at SWORD.

There is a daily pick-up and delivery service to and from each university. Journal articles are delivered either in paper or by fax. While the depository is not primarily designed for direct access by the user, a reading room with tables and computer access to OhioLINK is available to those who wish to use the premises.

Economy of cost makes the concept of regional depositories one of the more viable alternative solutions to future space problems.

15

COLLECTION MANAGEMENT AND DOCUMENT DELIVERY

Many times, plans for a new facility or merger change. The new facility may be put on hold for a decade (not unheard of in academia). In these circumstances, the situation which instigated the need for the move changes drastically. While in this facility, which may become permanent, alternative solutions to space problems should be carefully considered and implemented. This chapter suggests some alternative solutions.

ZERO GROWTH THROUGH WEEDING

The concept of zero growth through regular weeding is an appropriate solution for some libraries. Institutions where only the most current information is required to serve the information needs of the library user can utilize this strategy. It is not appropriate for institutions where an archival collection is required.

For the strategy of a zero growth collection to be successful weeding policies must be clearly stated and the librarian must be persistent in applying the policies. A strong commitment to the concept by all library staff members is necessary. The library user must understand this concept as well. Written criteria must be available that explain clearly what will be deselected and when it will be deselected. Library constituents should be informed of these criteria.

CONVERSION TO OTHER FORMATS

Many libraries have overcome space problems through conversion from print resources to alternative formats. One of the most well known alternative formats is microform.

Journal collections may be the fastest growing section of a library collection. The majority of journals now in print are available commercially in microform. Many libraries opt not to bind their print journals but to purchase replacements for their print journal in microform as these become available. The print sources are then discarded. Some libraries have the resources to microform their own journals and other document collections.

The popularity of CD-ROMs (Compact Disk Read-Only Memory) is proving to be a space saver for many facilities. One CD-ROM can contain the information found in 250 000 pages, 1650 floppy disks, 20 filing cabinets, or 12 bookcases. Even the smallest library now can provide multi-volume encyclopaedic sets, major reference sources, hundreds of indexing and abstracting sources in the space that it takes to house one personal computing work station with a CD-ROM drive. To see the breadth and depth of resources on CD-ROM consult *CD-ROMs in Print*, an annual publication.

Internet access to full text electronic resources is also helping some libraries to overcome space problems. If electronic access can fulfil the library user's needs and the space problem is critical, discarding the paper copies becomes possible.

DOCUMENT DELIVERY SERVICES

The rapid growth of journal collections is the culprit that creates the space problem for many libraries. Document delivery services may offer some libraries relief in this area. Traditional interlibrary loan services are slow, labour intensive, and expensive to operate. Copyright law also limits interlibrary loan requests for recent articles from the same journal title. Document delivery services are proving to be reliable and quick. Most of these services also handle the copyright compliance fees which are added into the cost of the document. There are numerous types of document delivery services. Major libraries may offer their own commercial document delivery service such as the British Library Document Supply Centre (which overwhelmingly dominates the UK market). Numerous document services own their own collections such as Chemical Abstracts Document Delivery Service or UMI Article Clearinghouse. Some document suppliers use the collections of other libraries such as The Information Store or Information Express. Additionally, there are the hybrid services which offer services other than just document delivery such as The Uncover Company. There are suppliers which offer direct access to full text or full image of documents such as Power Pages or ADONIS.

Some of these services focus their collection to highly specialized areas, many are more general in nature. A thorough investigation of these services could identify the service or services that would best fulfil your needs.

16

LOOKING TO THE FUTURE

❖

A move is an opportunity to examine the presumptions upon which the particular collections and services are built and to look ahead to the coming decades. It is a fitting time to evaluate how goals for the future might be accommodated in today's library plan. Which library services are likely to be expanded? Which might be discarded? What new equipment might be added? Is the collection likely to grow at the same pace or will electronic access replace the printed word? What size staff will be needed and what prerequisites would staff have to bring to their job? Will libraries continue to be the repository of information resources?

EDUCATION

The growing need for a well-schooled, informed and skilled workforce is likely to cause a further increase in student populations. Adults will return to college for schooling and training due to economic restructuring in industry. Rapidly changing technology and continually changing job content will lead to an increased demand for life-long learning programmes for adults. As the demand for advanced schooling rises so does the requirement for up-to-date library resources, services and study facilities.

TECHNOLOGY

Technology has brought about changes that could scarcely have been anticipated as recently as ten years ago. New and novel formats, delivery methods and transmission systems have been introduced. Connectivity via modem or the internet have broadened access to gateways and area net-works. Technology will continue to act as the major catalyst of change.

PUBLISHING TRENDS

Traditional publication output has stayed competitive with innovations in the past, a trend that is likely to continue into the next decade. Growing costs in serials and other types of publications will strain library budgets and force choices on how to apportion funding: how much to spend on elec-tronic innovations and how much on maintaining traditional collections and their housing. Electronic access has been a source of great enrichment. Electronic access is like a door into a house full of treasures. The treasures are still in demand and are likely to remain so for some time.

IMPACT OF FUTURE TRENDS

Difficult though it may be to forecast coming trends in today's rapidly changing technological environment, there are some precautions that can be taken in the design of a new library.

○   *Adopt an open-ended design approach.* It will lend itself to changes in the library's future spatial arrangement. It will provide an oppor-tunity to modify space configurations and make possible the reposi-tioning of such major library areas as the information hub, reader spaces, furniture, equipment and stacks according to the demands of the hour.

○   *Cluster service points* in the vicinity of where staff are working so that a reduction in personnel does not create a major inconvenience or inefficiency.

○   *Hire personnel capable of learning* new technological innovations and flexible enough to accept them as part of the daily work routine.

○   *Spotlight the information hub/reference resource centre* as the focal point of the library. Here access is provided to information via gate-ways connecting users to library catalogues all over the world, to databases listing citations, abstracts and full-text documents and to user-initiated document delivery.

○   *Plan for a library that is open to innovation* and can be adjusted to future changes cost-effectively.

REFERENCES

Ardis, Susan B., *Library Without Walls: Plug In and Go* (Washington, DC: Special Libraries Association, 1944).

Bayne, Pauline. S., 'The "Do-It-Yourself" Move for a 1.5 Million-Volume Library', *College and Research Libraries* 51: 55–6 (January 1990).

Boss, Richard W., *Telecommunications for Library Management* (White Plains, New York and London: Knowledge Industry Publications, Inc., 1985).

Bowker, R.R., *The Bowker Annual of Library and Trade Almanac* (New Jersey: R.R. Bowker, 1990).

Brawne, Michael, *Libraries: Architecture and Equipment* (New York, Washington and London: Praeger Publishers, 1970).

Bright, Franklin F., *Planning for a Movable Compact Shelving System* (Chicago and London: American Library Association, 1991).

Brin, Beth and Elissa Cochran, 'Access and Ownership in the Academic Environment: One Library's Progress Report', *Journal of Academic Librarianship* 20(4): 207–12 (September 1994).

British Standards Recommendations for Storage and Exhibition of Archival Documents: BS5454 (London: British Standards Institution, 1989).

CD-ROMS in Print 1994: An International Guide to CD-ROM, CD-1, 3DO, MMDC, CD32, Multimedia and Electronic Book Products (Westport, CT: Mecklermedia Corporation, 1994).

Chappell, David, *Standard Letters for Building Contractors* (London: Architectural Press, 1987).

Chepesiuk, R., 'An Anatomy of a Move', *Wilson Library Bulletin* pp. 32–5 (June 1991).

Cohen, Aaron and Elaine Cohen, *Designing and Space Planning for*

Libraries: A Behavioral Guide (New York and London: R. R. Bowker Company, 1979).

'Commercial Document Delivery: Vendor Selection Criteria', *Computers in Libraries* 14(9): 14 (October, 1994).

Cunha, George D. M., *Conservation of Library Materials: A Manual and Bibliography on the Care, Repair and Restoration of Library Materials* (Metuchen, N.J.: The Scarecrow Press, Inc., 1967).

Ellis, Judith Compton, 'Planning and Executing a Major Bookshift/Move Using an Electronic Spreadsheet', *College and Research Libraries News* 49: pp. 283–7 (May 1988).

Ellsworth, Ralph E., *Planning for Academic Library Buildings* (Metuchen, NJ: The Scarecrow Press, Inc., 1973).

Etter, Zana C., 'Impact of Curriculum Revision on Media Collection', *Special Libraries* 86: 83–90 (Spring 1995).

Fitt, Stephen, 'Moving Fully-Loaded Stacks Inexpensively', *College and Research Libraries News* 50(1): 19–21 (January 1989).

Foos, Donald D. and Nancy C. Pack, *How Libraries Must Comply With the American With Disabilities Act* (Phoenix, AZ: Oryx Press, 1992).

Fraley, Ruth A. and Carol Lee Anderson, *Library Space Planning* 2nd edn (New York and London: Neal-Schuman Publishers, Inc., 1985 and 1990).

Freifeld, Roberta and Caryl Masyr, *Space Planning* (Washington, DC: Special Libraries Association, 1991).

Galvin, Hoyt R. and Kathryn A. Devereaux, *Planning a Library Building: The Major Steps* (Chicago: American Library Association, 1955).

Gawrecki, Drahoslav, *Compact Library Shelving* (Chicago: American Library Association, 1968).

Hamilton, P. and P. Hindman, 'Moving a Library Collection', *Public Libraries* 26(1): pp. 4–7 (Spring 1987).

Hudson, Barry J., 'CD-ROM Network Access: Problems, Pitfalls and Perils', *CD-ROM Professional* 8(3): pp. 98–108 (March 1995).

Jackson , Mary E., 'Resource Sharing and Document Delivery in the 1990s: An Introduction', *Wilson Library Bulletin* 67(6): 35–6, 110 (February 1993).

Jackson, Mary E. and Karen Croneis, *Uses of Document Delivery Services,* ARL Spec Kit #204 (Washington, DC: Association of Research Libraries, 1994).

Kaufman, John E., *IES Lighting Handbook* (New York, NY: Illuminating Engineering Society of North America, 1987).

Kellerman, Lydia Suzanne, 'Moving Fragile Materials: Shrink-Wrapping at Penn State', *Collection Management* 18(1–2):117–28 (1993).

Kurkul, D. L., 'The Planning, Implementation, and Movement of an Academic Library Collection', *College and Research Libraries* 44(4): 220–34 (July 1983).

Kurosman, K., 'Document Delivery: A Comparison of Commercial Document Suppliers and Interlibrary Loan Services', *College and Research Libraries* 55(2): 129–39 (March 1994).

Ladley, Barbara, 'Questions to Ask ... When Choosing a Moving Company', *The Bottom Line* 1(4): 8 (1987).

Laffoon, Carolyn, Graham T. Richardson and Wilton N. Melhorn, 'Relocating a Science Library: How to Cope with Plans Gone Awry', *Science and Technology Libraries* 12(1): 91–7 (Autumn 1991).

Lushington, Nolan and Willis N. Mills, Jr, *Libraries Designed for Users* (Syracuse, NY: Gaylord Professional Publications, 1979).

Martin, Ron G., *Libraries for the Future: Planning Buildings that Work* (Chicago and London: American Library Association, 1992).

Medical Library Association, *Minimum Standards for Health Sciences Libraries in Hospitals* (Chicago: Medical Library Association, 1984).

Meinke, Darrel M., 'Pulling the Rug Out from Under the Stacks (Revisited)', *College and Research Libraries News* 49(5): pp. 288–9 (May 1988).

Meltzer, E., 'Successfully Moving the Library – Temporarily', *College and Research Libraries News* 54(10): pp. 557–60 (November 1993).

Metcalf, Keyes D., Philip D. Leighton and David C. Weber, *Planning Academic and Research Library Buildings* (Chicago and London: American Library Association, 1986).

Moeckel, Lisa E., 'Managing Staff with Dual Assignments: Challenge for the 1990s', *Library Administration and Management* 17(3): 181–4 (Summer 1993).

Moreland, Virginia F., 'Moving a Library Collection: Impact on Staff Morale', *Journal of Academic Librarianship* 19(1): 8–11 (March 1993).

Muller, Robert H., 'Economics of Compact Book Shelving', in *Reader on the Library Building*, edited by H. B. Schell, (Englewood, CO: Microcard Edition Books, 1975) pp. 292–300.

Myers, Charles, 'A Mover that only Moves Libraries', *American Libraries* 23(4): pp. 332–3 (April 1992).

Myller, Rolf, *The Design of the Small Public Library* (New York and London: R. R. Bowker, 1966).

Nilsen, Kirsti, 'Collection Development Issues of Academic Libraries: Converging or Diverging', *Collection Building* 13(4): 9–17 (1994).

Orr, James M., *Designing Library Buildings for Activity* (London: Andre Deutsch Limited, 1972).

Pierce, William S., *Furnishing the Library Interior* (New York and Basel: Marcel Dekker, Inc., 1980).

Planning Barrier Free Libraries: A Guide for Renovation and Construction of Libraries Serving Blind and Physically Handicapped Readers (Washington, DC: The Library of Congress, 1981).

Ramsey, Charles G., *Architectural Graphic Standards* 8th edn (New York: Wiley, 1992).

Reed, Lawrence L. and Rodney Erickson, 'Weeding: A Quantitative and Qualitative Approach', *Library Acquisitions: Practice and Theory* 17: 175–81 (Summer 1993).

Rizzo, Joe, 'Ten Ways to Look at a Library', *American Libraries* 23(4): pp. 322–4, 326 (April 1992).

Roth, B. G., 'Moving a Medical Center Library', *Special Libraries* 76(1): 31–4 (Winter 1985).

Sam, Sherrie and Jean A. Major, 'Compact Shelving of Circulating Collections', *College and Research Libraries News* 54(1): pp. 11–12 (January 1993)

Sommer, Robert, 'Reading Areas on College Libraries', *Libraries Quarterly* 38(3): 249–60 (July 1968).

Tennant, Roy, John Ober and Anne Grodzing, *Crossing the Internet Threshold: An Instructional Handbook* 2nd edn (Berkeley, CA: Library Solutions Press, 1994).

Thompson, Godfrey, *Planning and Design of Library Buildings* 3rd edn (London: Butterworth Architecture, 1989).

Trezza, Alphonse F., ed., *Library Buildings:Innovations for Changing Needs* (Chicago: American Library Association, 1972).

Truesdell, Cheryl B., 'Is Access a Viable Alternative to Ownership? A Review of Access Performance', *Journal of Academic Librarianship* 20(4): 200–206 (September 1994)

Tucker, Dennis C., *From Here to There: Moving a Library* (Bristol, Indiana: Wyndham Hall Press, 1987).

Turock, Betty J., *Creating a Financial Plan: How To Do It Manual for Librarians* (New York: Neal-Schuman Publishers, 1992).

2001: A Space Reality Strategies for Obtaining Funding for New Library Space, SPEC KIT 200 compiled by Paula T. Kaufman and Aubrey H. Mitchell (Washington, DC: Association of Research Libraries, 1994).

Wells, Marianna S. and Richard A. Spohn, 'Planning, Implementation, and Benefits of Merging the Geology and Physics Libraries into a Combined Renovated Facility at the University of Cincinnati', *Proceedings 25th Meeting of the Geoscience Information Society, held from 20 October – 1 November 1990 held at Dallas, TX* 20: 173–83 (Alexandria, VA: Geoscience Information Society, 1990).

Wells, Marianna S. and Rosemary Young, 'Making Your Move and Getting it Right', *Special Libraries* 85(3): 145–53 (Summer 1994).

Woodson, Wesley E., *Human Factors Design Handbook* 2nd edn (New York, NY: Wiley, 1992).

INDEX

Preservation Management

Policies and Practices in British Libraries

John Feather, Graham Matthews and Paul Eden

Much has happened in libraries and information in the last ten years and preservation and conservation issues have developed accordingly. The authors carried out a survey of around 500 British libraries to study preservation management practices over that period and the results of this questionnaire are the basis of this book. In analysing the responses it was clear that the fundamental issues about the access to and use of books were being addressed; preservation and retention of materials and media being the foundation of access.

Having put the research into its historical context, the book moves on to the findings about management attitudes and practices. Policy issues are considered, and some of the national and international prescriptive policy documents issued by professional organizations are compared with those from the British libraries. The differences between the two form the basis of suggestions about how individual libraries might develop preservation policies and also what national policies could be considered.

This is a book that will enable all librarians from all sectors to understand the importance and nature of preservation policies and to begin to create or improve their own.

Gower

Records Management Handbook

2nd Edition

Ira A Penn, Gail B Pennix and Jim Coulson

Records Management Handbook is a complete guide to the practice of records and information management. Written from a multi-media perspective and with a comprehensive systems design orientation, the authors present proven management strategies for developing, implementing and operating a "21st century" records management programme. Where most available titles are biased toward dealing with inactive records, this book gives a balanced treatment for all phases of the record's life cycle, from creation or receipt through to ultimate disposition.

The *Records Management Handbook* is a practical reference for use by records managers, analysts, and other information management professionals, which will aid decision-making, improve job performance, stimulate ideas, help avoid legal problems, minimize risk and error, save time and reduce expense.

Special features of the second edition include • new chapters on record media, active records systems and records disposition • new information on management strategies and programme implementation • revised guidance and material on records appraisal and record inventorying • expanded and increased information on retention scheduling, records storage and electronic forms.

Gower